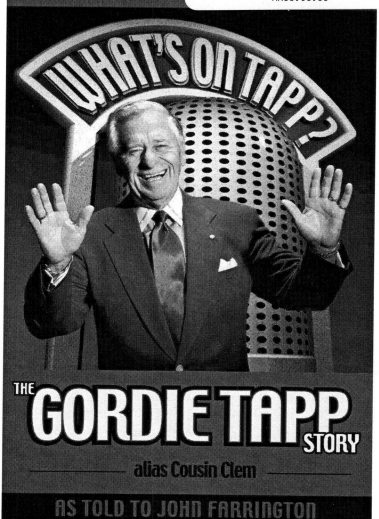

WHAT'S ON TAPP?

THE GORDIE TAPP STORY

alias Cousin Clem

AS TOLD TO JOHN FARRINGTON

Published by
farringtonmedia

in co-operation with

Note for Librarians: A cataloguing record for this book is available from Library and Archives Canada at www.collectionscanada.ca/amicus/index-e.html
ISBN 1-4251-0656-0

Printed in Victoria, BC, Canada. Printed on paper with minimum 30% recycled fibre. Trafford's print shop runs on "green energy" from solar, wind and other environmentally-friendly power sources.

TRAFFORD
PUBLISHING™

Offices in Canada, USA, Ireland and UK

Book sales for North America and international:
Trafford Publishing, 6E–2333 Government St.,
Victoria, BC V8T 4P4 CANADA
phone 250 383 6864 (toll-free 1 888 232 4444)
fax 250 383 6804; email to orders@trafford.com
Book sales in Europe:
Trafford Publishing (UK) Limited, 9 Park End Street, 2nd Floor
Oxford, UK OX1 1HH UNITED KINGDOM
phone 44 (0)1865 722 113 (local rate 0845 230 9601)
facsimile 44 (0)1865 722 868; info.uk@trafford.com
Order online at:
trafford.com/06-2414

10 9 8 7 6 5

DEDICATION

I am dedicating this story of my life to the people who mean the most to me - my wife, Helen, our four children and their loved ones. I love you all.

My Mom and Dad who taught me well.

My childhood sweetheart and wife of more than 60 years, Helen, who has been my greatest inspiration from the very beginning. She still laughs at my jokes.

My daughter Barbara, her husband Alan and their children Jennifer, Stephanie and Brad.

My daughter Kathleen, her husband Ed and their children Derek and Craig.

My daughter Joan, her husband Frank and her children Joshua and Joel.

My son Jeffrey, his wife Bernie and his children Kim, Kristi and twins Matthew and Ashley.

And the great-grandchildren who are helping to keep us young.

TABLE OF CONTENTS

Library and Archives Canada / Gordie Tapp Collection

"Gordie Tapp? Man, he's something else again. I look at him - he looks at me - and I just start laughing. He's the funniest!"

Johnny Cash

ACKNOWLEDGMENTS

I would especially like to thank people who have helped me and made a difference in my life:

- Stan Jacobson, a life-long friend and a great producer.

- Sam Lovullo, the producer of *Hee Haw*, who sent along some nice comments for this book.

- Lorne Greene who encouraged me to go back to high school before accepting me in his broadcasting college.

- All those who used to listen to me in my early years at radio stations in Niagara Falls, Guelph and Hamilton.

- Tom Darling who persuaded me to switch from big band and easy listening music to country and western music - and then recognized I had a rapport with the country music fans . . . even before I realized it myself!

- Sandy Liles, of Gaylord Program Services, who helped get the *Hee Haw* show pictures for this book.

- Debbie Brentnell and all those who helped me to retrieve information and relive so many memories in my scrapbooks that are now in the National Archives of Canada in Ottawa.

- Lynda Barnett, Library Coordinator, CBC Design Library and Still Photo Collection, Toronto and Brenda Carol, Media Librarian, CBC Still Photo Collection, who provided many pictures for this book from the CBC files.

- Bob Cole, the former CBC cameraman who contributed some unsolicited words for this book that I really appreciate.

- The genuine people of all creeds and colours who have laughed along with me for more than 60 years, welcomed me with open arms into their culture and their life . . . and made us feel good about what we were doing.

- I would be remiss not to mention how kind my local newspapers have been to me over the years - in Burlington, Milton, Hamilton and Kitchener.

- John Farrington, the editor who helped me get my thoughts and writings arranged for this book.

- Transcription of all my tapes by Adair Thompson, of Oakville, Ontario and Graeme Thompson, of Liverpool, Nova Scotia.

- All the Canadian Forces based in Canada and all over the world. What a pleasure it has been performing for them.

ACKNOWLEDGMENTS

Dismatsek Photo, Hamilton

Michael Nikas, a professional photographer who owns Dismatsek in Hamilton, Ontario, has kindly allowed his picture of Gordie to be used on the cover of this book.

Publication design: farringtonmedia, Oakville, Ontario

Cover design: www.ANDREWtheARTIST.com, Brussels, Belgium

Published by

farringtonmedia

2007 Erika Court

Oakville, Ontario, Canada, L6M 4R4

Tel,. 905-469-4201 Fax: 905-469-4202

email: john@farringtonmedia.com www.farringtonmedia.com

in co-operation with

TRAFFORD

6E - 2333 Government Street

Victoria, B.C., Canada, V8T 4P4

www.trafford.com

Gordie Tapp

One of Gordie's favourite pictures . . . taken by an old friend Tommy Hunter . . . on the day Gordie caught a 148 1/2-pound blue marlin in Florida.

INTRODUCTION

By John Farrington

I've heard hundreds of jokes in my life – but can't remember one.

Gordie Tapp has heard thousands – and he can remember them all. Even those he heard back in the schoolyard – and he's 84 years-old.

Gordie has a story for every occasion . . . for any circumstance.

He doesn't write down the jokes – never has. He just has a tremendous mind for storing jokes – and a fabulous retrieval system.

He's never stuck for a word to say and can usually make a joke out of anything.

This is why comedian Foster Brooks introduced Gordie to U.S. President Gerald Ford as "the world's funniest story-teller."

Not only does he never miss the punch-line, he has a way of getting to it in a pleasant, easy-going manner and a voice that is radio-trained, clear, easy to understand.

Did you want that told in a Newfie accent . . . a Jewish accent . . . how about French . . . the Deep South . . . even deeper south, Mexican . . . English . . . Scottish . . . Irish? There's more. Lots more.

He has been able to tell a story in a dialect and with an accent that even the locals can't detect as false.

But that's not surprising, everything's genuine about Gordie. He has lived a life – so far, at any rate, after all he's only 84 – that we all should live.

He's 84 years-young, not 84 years-old.

He could easily pass for a 65-year-old. His wife, Helen, has been blessed with the same ageless gene.

They not only look as though they haven't started picking up their pension yet, they both act like they are too young to claim government old-age security cheques.

Gordie was still roller-blading up to two years ago when he was 82.

He was 80 when he sold his Harley-Davidson motorcycle – not because he can't ride it any more . . . he just doesn't trust others on the road. Helen rode

9

Introduction

Harley until she was 75.

They look after themselves with regular visits to the doctor and the dentist.

They live in the country in a beautiful bungalow on a farm acreage.

Gordie still loves to ride horses and Helen gets around the property in a golf cart since her hip surgery.

They are both Toronto Blue Jays fans and try not to miss an inning on their big-screen television.

But they are far from couch potatoes.

Gordie still likes to golf. Helen's game is bridge. They both love to go out to dinner with long-time friends, whom they treasure.

They have been married for 63 years and still like each other's company. They have four children, the oldest is nearing 60 and the youngest just had his 50th birthday . . . 11 grandchildren and seven – soon-to-be eight – great-grandchildren.

Gordie still works, telling jokes and singing songs on stages all over North America. His audiences are mainly seniors.

Helen always likes to travel with him, and be in the audience, especially when he is playing in the United States or another province.

Maybe she's like me and likes to hear the stories over and over and admire the inventiveness of her husband as he switches bottom lines, punch-lines and story lines to fit the audience or the day.

Writing this book has been a delight, but somewhat of a challenge trying to maintain his story-telling ways. That's why you'll see a lot of "he saids," "she saids" and "I saids."

If you want to see and hear Gordie go through a 45-minute routine, he's offering a 'free' DVD at the end of this book. All you pay for is the shipping and handling.

Hee Haw, the television show he starred in for more than a quarter-of-a-century, that was watched by 50 million people every week, is making a comeback in reruns now that CMT (Country Music Television) has secured the rights.

A whole new generation will be exposed to Gordie's wit – and he's the kind of comedian who you can sit and listen to with your mother. Some of the material is a little risqué, but there are no dirty jokes . . . and absolutely no swearing.

But then, what would you expect from a comedian who almost became a Baptist minister.

I won't spoil the book. It's filled with many great stories.

I hope you'll get to enjoy and admire Gordie as I did. You'll also see how this delightful couple brings that old-time saying to reality – behind every great man there is an even greater woman!

It's been a pleasure to get to know Gordie and Helen. Now it's your turn.

Sincerely,

John Farrington

Editor and Publisher

February 2007

John Farrington has been a journalist for 48 years, starting in his English hometown weekly in Crewe, Cheshire, in July 1958. He worked in England for seven years before emigrating to Canada in 1965. He has been Managing Editor at several Canadian newspapers, including Kirkland Lake, Peterborough, Sarnia, Lethbridge, and Sudbury and Publisher and General Manager in Nanaimo, Timmins. Cornwall and the Multicom group in Toronto. He was National Editorial Consultant for Thomson Newspapers from 1980-1982 and Northern Ontario Journalist of the Year in 1990. He collaborated with Stompin' Tom Connors on his Number 1 autobiography. Currently he operates his own company, farringtonmedia, editing and writing books, and produces a quarterly in-flight magazine for Air Creebec, serving the Cree communities in the James Bay area of Ontario and Quebec.

Foreword

Producer/director Stan Jacobson, right, who has written the Foreword for this book, with The Man in Black, Johnny Cash.

FOREWORD

By Stan Jacobson

Gordie Tapp has always made me laugh, ever since I first watched him cavorting around as the host of CBC's very popular television show, *Country Hoedown.*

Over the years he's made me laugh at the numerous lunches and dinners we had and as host or guest star on many of the television specials I produced.

In 1969, we were both in Nashville, Tennessee at the same time. He was co-starring in the hugely successful country comedy series *Hee Haw* and I was producing the Johnny Cash television show.

We often met for breakfast at the Ramada Inn and before long I'd be laughed out for the day.

However, there was one day I didn't laugh and actually came close to tears. In 1960 I was asked to join the writing staff of *Country Hoedown.* I thought that discretion was the better part of valour and so I copied Gordie's opening remarks from the last season's first show. Now the first time Gordie used the script was the run through - an informal dress rehearsal. Sitting in the empty bleachers I watched Gordie read from the script: "Howdy friends and neighbours and welcome to another season of your favourite show and mine, *Country Hoedown!*" He stopped, raised his left hand holding the script and shouted for all to hear, "who wrote this shit?" I prayed a hole would open up in the bleachers and I would disappear for ever.

When Gordie saw my reaction he came over to me with a big smile on his face, "Just kidding, Stan . . . . that's my way of welcoming you to the show, pal." And pals we became.

It is difficult to describe Gordie Tapp. He's so many things: a comedian, story-teller par excellence, a wonderful humanitarian and an academy award prankster. On a night flight out west, Gordie and a group of entertainers were headed for British Columbia to entertain our Canadian troops over the Christmas holiday season. One of the performers was King Ganam, *Country Hoedown's* expert fiddle player. Among his other attributes was his enormous gullibility.

Foreword

As the airplane took off, Gordie told King to be very careful when he goes into the lavatory. He explained that the ground crew unhooks the lavatory floor and the refuse drops into a dumpster. He went on to explain that one side of the floor is hinged and the other has the closing hook and sometimes the ground crew doesn't close it securely.

Now, everyone on the airplane was in on this prank, except, of course, the King.

It is now about 3 a.m. and no one has gone to the lavatory. Finally, Ganam gets up and slowly makes his way towards the head. The rest pretend that they're sleeping. King slowly opens the door and holds on to the door frame, stretches his right leg into the lavatory and began stomping on the lavatory floor. Never before and never again will such laughter be heard at 38,000 feet over the Rocky Mountains.

Before joining *Country Hoedown,* I was asked to observe the last three shows of the current season. On one of these shows, I have never before or since been around such pandemonium.

It was the closing number and Gordie made his entrance as Cousin Clem - his hillbilly alter-ego, along with a porcine companion . . . a little piglet. Gordie was directing this little guy with a long wooden staff. Unfortunately, the piglet didn't take direction too well, so Gordie gave him a slight whack on his bottom. The piglet retaliated with a bowel movement. Not an ordinary BM, but one that looked like it was shot out of a cannon and right in the direction of the band. All hell broke loose and mercifully the show got off the air.

Believe me Gordie isn't all fun and games. I don't know of any other performer who's logged more miles to entertain our troops all over the world, not to mention the thousands of hours he has performed for the sick and infirmed.

A few years ago I had the honour of producing a salute to Gordie in recognition of his 50 years in show business. The event was hosted by his old *Country Hoedown* pal, Tommy Hunter. Many of his *Hoedown* and *Hee Haw* friends performed before a sold-out audience at Kitchener's Centre in the Square theatre. Gordon Lightfoot, The Hames Sisters, Roy Clark, Grandpa Jones and Don Harron to name a few. Finally, Gordie was called up on stage and received a standing ovation that was so loud and emotional his legs almost buckled.

But he recovered and sang a song that he wrote for this special occasion, *Friends* an affirmation of the importance of his friends he met along the way and their importance to him.

Gordie Tapp

Some say that laughter adds years to one's life - and so if you have the good fortune to meet Gordie Tapp, I suggest you stay very close to him and I promise you'll be laughing for a long, long time.

Stan Jacobson

Stan Jacobson has been a producer and director of television shows for more than half-a-century. He was producer-director-writer of The Johnny Cash Show on ABC in the late 60s and early 70s, doing 60 shows in all. He wrote 39 Country Hoedown shows in 1960, where he got to know Gordie. Stan's impressive credits over the years include producing and directing shows with Hank Snow, Wayne and Shuster, Burton Cummings, Bill Murray, the King of Kensington, for CBC, the 1968 Andy Williams Christmas Show for NBC, Al Hirt's New Orleans Special in 1972 for CBS, Dave Garroway At Large special for 20th Century Fox in 1972, the Arte Johnson Christmas Special for CTV in 1973. He did many Miss Canada and Miss Teen Canada pageants for CTV, and was producer, director and head-writer for the SkyDome opening ceremonies in Toronto in 1989.

Gordie Tapp

Gordie and Helen on their 43rd wedding anniversary

1

Entertaining at age 5

I was born on Sunday June the 4th 1922, in Bethesda Hospital, London, Ontario, to Gladys Ilene Tapp, nee Bedford and Robert Frederick Tapp. My mother said I took after my father, my father said I took after my mother, but I fooled them both, I jumped out of the crib and took after the nurse. Well, if you're going to be a comic, I guess you'd better start at an early age.

In this book you'll notice that whenever I get an opportunity to bring in a joke, a punch line, even a little bit of levity, I'll do it. It's not that I make light of my life, or life in general, but I don't want to be deathly serious. You'll get the truth, but I hope you'll have as much fun reading about my nine decades on this planet as I have had living them.

We lived south of London, Ontario, and when I was four years of age my mother had my sister Bernice. Bernice was born in April, so for several months of the year I was four years older than her, and the rest of the time I was three years older than her. You know what it's like as kids. We made a lot of that age difference. Three or four years difference in age is nothing, but when you are young and trying to establish yourself you go after any leverage you can find.

When I look back there was no need for all this nonsense. But then we were kids. And we wouldn't be kids if we didn't fight for attention. I don't think any punches were thrown in those kiddie struggles, it was all kid's stuff. Identities

Entertaining at age 5

were being created. Little personalities were being molded. Feelings I am sure were hurt by silly things as we kids made mountains out of the proverbial molehills, but I doubt we ever gave mom or dad any real trouble.

Truth is we were well loved. Always pressed and dressed. We reciprocated by always being well behaved. At least that's my take on it. And I'm sticking with that.

At the age of five my father taught me how to play the harmonica. He would play it and I'd sit and listen to him, and one day I picked up the harmonica and played a song called *There's a Rainbow Around My Shoulder* and *It Fits Me Like a Glove*, I can remember even the lyrics. They were surprised when I played it. I picked up the harmonica very quickly.

George Jarvis was the principal of Odell School, the three-room school which I attended. While I was there in kindergarten or Grade 1, I forget now because we started at five years of age in those days, I joined the Odell School harmonica band. That was my first experience in show business. We played school concerts and Rotary clubs.

I remember one time we went to the Masonic Hall in downtown London, across from the Beal Technical School. Of course, being just a tiny lad, I got lost. I can remember the panic running from room to room trying to find the principal Mr. Jarvis, who was also the leader of our group.

One of the things I remember most about playing in the band, we had white duck pants and little red jackets with white piping. We weren't poor, but we weren't well off, and I didn't have clothes like that. I can remember how proud I was of that little outfit. It was really something to be able to wear that, because mother wouldn't let me wear it for anything but our harmonica band presentations.

I always wanted to entertain, I would imitate everything. Sounds of birds, sounds of trains, I would make train sounds with my feet. I don't know whether I could still do it today or not. My grandmother was a very devout Baptist and had a minister who was Scottish. I used to imitate him. I can remember my grandmother calling me to come in and imitate McGinnly, the minister.

I would imitate schoolteachers. When they'd leave the room I'd get up on the desk and talk like them. If we ever had a supply teacher, I used to talk with an accent. I'd be Scottish, or English or Irish. I was always good at accents. Of course, I've been living with them ever since. When I would get up in class and do an accent, the kids would all laugh because they knew that I didn't have that accent actually. The supply teacher didn't know, so it was ironic really.

You know, I've always wanted to make people laugh. My wife has said that I'd lose a friend to get a laugh.

I don't think I would ever do that. Friends are too precious to me. But you get the idea. I love to have friends and I enjoy laughing. And when I can make others laugh that makes me feel good. It actually fires me up to do more jokes, tell more stories.

I took guitar lessons from Edith Hill Adams and Erwin Edwards, but was never a good musical student. I learned more playing with other guys, picking up chords. That's about what I still do.

I use my music knowledge more as a means of presenting comedy when I do the Cousin Clem thing.

But back in those school days, I used to accompany my sister who played harmonica. I had a holder around my neck for my harmonica. We used to sing in harmony and yodel. The things you remember.

2

Family made 'dough' from bread

I was watching television one time and they did a show on family trees. It was a program which talked about people's past and led them to recognise the attributes of their family and how they came to be. I thought, well that's rather interesting. I really got into the program and learned some very interesting facts about my family.

For instance, my ancestors lived in biblical times. In fact, I had a relative at the Last Supper. He wasn't in the picture because he wasn't at the head table. As a matter of fact he sat at table four. And by golly, can you believe it, he won the centerpiece.

Then I had family living in the Renaissance period: I had a relative who worked with Michelangelo when Michael was painting the Sistine Chapel ceiling. While Michael was doing that, my relative was doing the bookshelves and the cupboards.

Another relative was a perverted Greek shepherd, Popodopolis Tapp and he actually married the black sheep of the family.

We had several relatives named for famous people; there was Christopher Columbus Tapp, he was the second explorer to get into Florence. Unfortunately, Florence's husband came home at the time and shot my relative as he was escaping through a northwest passage.

Gordie Tapp

I had a relative named Robinson Crusoe Tapp. Now, he didn't have a good man Friday, but he had a nice lady on Thursday.

And there was a relative called Paul Revere Tapp. He got drunk one night and rode through the streets of Vancouver on a horse, crying "The Chinese are coming! The Chinese are coming!"

And I had a relative named Dracula Tapp. He was a comedian. He wasn't a vampire, but all his jokes sucked.

And I guess that's about it for my family tree, up until now.

I have always liked that. I got the material from a very funny Italian comedian Dick Capri - that's not stealing, it's research. It's always good for a laugh wherever I go. But, of course, it's not my family. It's a great introduction though. At least I hope it got your attention because I think it is important for each of us to know where we came from. Is there anyone we particularly take after? Do we have any traits that were passed down through the generations, and even more specifically through the genes?

My family have been bakers for generations. My grandparents had 11 children - so that's a family of 13, a baker's dozen. I was never a baker, although I can make toast, sometimes without burning it! And you should see me boil water!

I like to think I got my story-telling talents from my great uncle, Herb Bedford. He would have a lot of accents and some neat expressions, like: Never stand when you can sit . . . never run when you can walk . . . never pass water without taking a drink. That last comment I always thought that he was saying never pass up an opportunity to take a drink, but I found out what he meant was that you should never take a pee without replenishing the water expelled.

One of my great-grandchildren, Avalon, has developed a knack of telling stories in dialect. Too many of my stories over the years, or just enough to carry on a learned trait? Whatever it is, I feel very satisfied – and obviously very proud - that one of our clan has picked up the knack of telling stories in dialect. She may never use it as a profession, but that's not important. Just to be able to tell stories, pass them on to her children and our family will be blessed for years to come, maybe even generations to come, learning about their heritage.

Please take a moment to read about my ancestors. If you haven't already tried to record your ancestors, take time and start doing your family genealogy. It's neat. It's something that you'll be glad you did. Certainly there will be family

Family made 'dough' from bread

in the future who will be happy you took the time. Maybe you will be easily able to see why you are like you are. Perhaps there will be a little grandson or granddaughter in the future who will be able to see that you were their inspiration.

Here's the real Tapp family:

James Darville Tapp (1847-1941), the third of seven children of George and Susannah Tapp, was born in Fillongley, a village in the North Warwickshire district of the county of Warwickshire, England.

Fillongley goes back to medieval times and I believe it was the site of two castles over the centuries. However, both castles were long gone before the start of the 16th century. The Parish church of St.. Mary and All Saints dates back to the 12th century and inside there are beautiful examples of stained glass from the 14th century. I don't know if there were any Tapps way back then, but it would be neat to know. That's a project for another day. For now, I'll go back just to grandfather's day.

Why my grandparents left this beautiful part of England, I don't know. It was during the Industrial Revolution in England and Fillongley was deep in the heart of what was to be later known as The Black Country, the green and beautiful land that became pocked by coal mines as rural gave way to urban, and Birmingham and Coventry blossomed nearby.

James emigrated to London, Ontario, and in 1872 he married a cousin, Alma Darville Tapp (1854-1918) daughter of James and Mary Ann Tapp who had emigrated to London earlier.

James and Alma later moved to a new, large, white brick house they had built on the south side of Emery Street, in Middlesex County.

James had learned to be a baker in Birmingham, England, prior to his marriage and he continued to practise the skills of the trade at his Emery Street residence, where he sold bread, buns and other baked and confectionery goods.

Their 11 children were James Darville Jr., Annie Susan, George William, Edward Arthur, William Edgar, Alma Florence (1885-1967) unmarried, Eleanor Frances 'Nell', Maude Mary (1890-1980) unmarried, Joseph Eustace (1893-1911) who died young, Francis Robert 'Frank' and Robert Frederick. Of the children, James Jr., Annie Sue, Edward, William, Alma and Frank were also bakers.

My father Robert (1900-1985), was the youngest. He married Gladys Ilene

Gordie Tapp

Gordie Tapp family photo

Look at that double-breasted jacket and very fashionable plus-fours. That's Gordie at about six or seven years old, with mom and dad and sister Bernice.

Bedford (1901-1987). They raised two children, Gordon Robert (Gordie, that's me) and Dorothy Bernice, who attended Odell School in Westminster Township. I was born in 1922, married Constance Helen Mair, who was also born in 1922. She was the daughter of Gordon and Constance (Lund) Mair,

23

Family made 'dough' from bread

Gordie Tapp family photo

Helen and Gordie at a wedding where Helen was a bridesmaid.

in 1944. We raised four children in the Burlington area of Ontario.

My sister, Bernice, born in 1926, married George Stiles (1922-1976). They raised three children in London.

Helen and I have been married for more than 60 years. It's been wonderful.

I know you all want to know when we first kissed – or when we decided that we were meant for each other. That's what these kind of biographical books are usually filled with.

But, you know, I am sorry to tell you that I am not the kiss and tell type, and neither is Helen. If we were, we couldn't tell you. Both of us forget the first kiss.

I can tell you that we met when we were both just 17. It was the summer of 1939 and I was driving home from a Baptist evening service in London, Ontario, with my buddy, Morley Scoyne, when I spotted Helen walking with a girl I knew from our church.

I stopped to give the two girls a ride and had Helen sit in the front seat with me and Morley got in the back with Helen's friend Grace. I had the gift of the gab back then, but just didn't know how to make small talk with Helen. So I told her all about the engine of the car we were riding in.

We went for five-cent ice cream cones. And I was head-over-heels about Helen right from the get-go. She looked like Deanna Durbin, who was the big film star of the day with her long, dark hair.

At home with Helen and the kids around one of our first television sets.

I liked the fact that she seemed intelligent. She told me later that she liked how outgoing I was and I liked Helen because she seemed to be a thinker and was quite quiet. I suppose we were opposites, but we really clicked.

When we started dating we loved to go dancing and in the summer we enjoyed going to the beach. I drove a grey 1928 Dort with a sign painted on the side that said "Don't laugh, Mother, Your daughter might be inside."

I went into the Army and on Christmas leave in 1942 we became engaged. I don't know what happened, but the engagement was called off and for a few

Family made 'dough' from bread

months we didn't see each other. I thought about Helen a lot during the time we were apart and then one day we bumped into each other on a London street.

I was determined I wasn't going to let her go again. I proposed in late summer and we were engaged for a second time in September 1943. We married in January 1944.

We struggled in those early years together. After all, we were both just 21 when we were married. I didn't have a job. Neither of us had any money. We had each other – and we had the commitment that we would look after each other until 'death do us part.' We believed that then. We struggled together. We dealt with problems together. We came up with solutions together. This is what the marriage commitment is all about.

I think that I am able to see the funny side of everything, so humour has been a great medicine for us.

We have four children – three girls and a boy. My first born, Barbara is 59. Kathleen is 56, Joanie, 54 and Jeffrey is 50. These kids have produced 11 grandchildren and seven great-grandchildren with one on the way.

Joanie is married to a mechanic and it is the second marriage for both of them. Joanie was divorced when she was quite young – raised two boys on her own, and did a marvellous job. They turned out to be fine young fellas. Her husband is a wonderful, wonderful guy. They're just so well suited. They love NASCAR, wear NASCAR clothes and go everywhere to the NASCAR races.

Jeffrey has been in the trucking business for at least 30 years. He was Canada's rep for J.B. Hunt for 11 years, they're one of the biggest in the world, second only to Schneider. I think Schneider's bigger because they have tankers. Jeffrey's now with Lakeside Logistics, an amazing company. They move in and they take over all of your shipping and receiving and free the company of all that. It's really quite an interesting organization, I guess it's being done a lot now. He's been with them a couple of years, his wife's with them too. She's with public relations and travels all over, visiting the various trucking companies that have a relationship with Lakeside and helps to keep them happy.

Kathleen, our second daughter, is the only one in show business. She is a lyric soprano – very popular in Toronto – sings with the Elmer Eiseler Singers and with the Toronto Amadeus Choir. She also teaches singing and has 25 students. She is married to Ed Mock, Technical Director of Ontario Place, they have two sons, Derek and Craig, both university graduates. She's a lovely girl, just like

Gordie Tapp

her mother.

Barbara, my oldest, has been married for – well she's 59, she's been married for quite a while. She's got children well into their 30s. We, fortunately, have built on property they own up in Rockwood, Ontario. So, it's kind of convenient, and she's a great gal, she means a lot to us.

My great-grandchildren are growing up fast. The oldest, Avalon, is Jennifer's daughter. Ella is Stephanie's daughter and she and Avalon vie for attention and make a great pair. Our other great-grandchildren are: Benjamin, Sebastian, Miranda, Deklan and Melody.

My oldest daughter Barbara was in nurse's training in Kitchener when she met and married a very handsome young man by the name of Rick Asmussen, whose father owned Asmussen Construction and is responsible for many of the beautiful buildings that are in the Kitchener area.

They were married for some time and had two daughters named Jennifer and Stephanie. One day when they were just babies, Rick left his mother, wife, and babies at their farm in Ayr, took off on an errand and was killed in an automobile accident.

It was very sudden, very sad.

Barbara remarried some time later and has a son by her second marriage, she had two children by her first.

We live very close to Barbara. We built on her farm and I have my horses there. We enjoy her as a daughter. We enjoy her as a person and certainly she's an outstanding member of our family.

She has a son, Brad, now 33, by her second husband, Alan Hails, who is a retired school teacher. He keeps busy at the farm. He's a woodworker, does a lot of jobs around the area. He's a good son-in-law. We're fortunate, all of our sons-in-law are all pretty good fellows.

I'd also like to make a special mention of my brother-in-law, John Mair, Helen's brother. We were close to the same age, and Jack - as we called him - studied violin. He was good enough to play for Fritz Chrysler, who was quite enthralled with the young man's ability and said with constant training and practice he could be a virtuoso.

That didn't mean much to Jack. However, he played second violin in the Toronto Symphony Orchestra and was the featured soloist in one concert. His

Family made 'dough' from bread

mother and father came from London to Toronto to see the performance. Jack got a standing ovation and his father asked him 'What did it feel like?' Jack said "I'd rather be fishing up at Colpoy Bay."

That was his attitude, but he was a clever musician. He stayed with the symphony for some time and then went to the National Arts Centre Orchestra in Ottawa, and he played first viola. But then he developed kind of a tightening of the sinews in his left hand, his fingering hand, and it delayed his playing for quite a length of time.

Finally, he had to give up playing altogether.

Jack joined the army in 1940 and came home safely at the end of the war. And I joined in 1942 and when I was discharged and got entrance into the Academy of Radio Arts, Jack and I lived together in Toronto.

He was studying then with Kathleen Parlow at the senior school at the Conservatory of Toronto.

Helen's brother, John Mair, played second violin with Toronto Symphony Orchestra.

I used to sleep in the morning and Jack would be up at six o'clock playing Bartock, or some fancy composer's music, that I never understood because it wasn't country or fiddle – well it was fiddle, but violin, and there's a difference.

Jack was in the second wave that landed at Juno Beach in World War II. How he went through all that and survived I don't know. I think the most serious injury he received was a cut on his finger. He was reconnaissance for the artillery and was continually in the front line because, as you know, those fellows had to be up front seeing what was going on in order to direct the firing of the artillery.

Anyway, Jack is gone, and we'll not forget him. We spent a lot of time together; did a lot fishing and lived close together for a good portion of his life.

Gordie and Helen and their children ready to cut the cake at their 50th wedding anniversary. From left, Barbara, Kathleen, Joan and Jeffrey.

Gordie Tapp

Gordie's first promo picture in Hollywood in 1969 - 'they sure know how to make you look good.''

3

Baptists wanted Gordie to be a minister

M y father was a very strict Baptist and he brought me up that way. It stood me in good stead in my business, I'm sure. But he had tunnel vision when it came to what was right and what was wrong. It made it very difficult for me in my teenage years because he wouldn't let me go to movies.

Regardless of that, he was a good man and provided for us, and that's what's important. I remember the church wanted me to go to the Toronto Bible Seminary and become a minister because I was outgoing as a youngster. This was told to my father, he came and told me. He was quite excited and thought it would be wonderful. I told him that I wasn't called to the ministry and I didn't think I should go. He was really very disappointed.

A few years later, when world famous evangelist Billy Graham was on our television show, *Hee Haw*, I told him the story of the church inviting me to become a minister and he was quite amused by it.

Later on I got a letter from Billy Graham inviting me to sit on the stage with him during his Crusade in Knoxville, Tennessee. I was unable to go because I was recording *Hee Haw* at the time, or filming.

Baptists wanted Gordie to be minister

I brought the letter home because I was proud of it and I showed it to my father and his reaction was unbelievable. He looked at it, read it and said to me, "Is this the real Billy Graham, Gord?" I said, "Yes, of course, what would make you ask that?" He said, "Why would he want a backslider like you to sit on the stage with him?" I said, "Tell it like it is, dad." That's the way he was.

He would have been pleased had I worked alongside him at the shoe factory where he was employed. I think that when I got out of the army he expected me to go back to the shoe factory. I don't think it ever crossed his mind that I might want to do something else.

The fact that I went back to finnish high school as a married man, what I should have done as a teenager, never really registered with him. I was a drop out and that was that. Perhaps he thought I had embarrassed him enough by not finishing high school in the normal course of events.

I am trying to make excuses for him now and I shouldn't be doing that. It's too bad I didn't talk to him at the time. But it really didn't matter to me then as much as it does now. Yes, even today, and I am 84 years-old I still think about the way my dad treated me. It's made me a better father because I have tried very hard not to make the same kinds of mistakes with my children.

Even when I had been successful on radio and television, he still wouldn't pay me any compliments. I never held a grudge. I just hoped that one day he would soften toward me. He never did.

When I went on the road to various concert dates in Ontario, I would rent a mobile home and I'd take mom and dad and my wife, Helen with me. Dad would never go to the shows, he'd always sit in the mobile home. Helen would come from the show and my dad would say, "Helen, is Gord out there telling dirty jokes?" He heard the people laughing, so he assumed it must be dirty jokes. Helen would say, "Oh no dad, you know he doesn't tell dirty jokes."

I don't know that he ever believed that. He never did see any of those live shows. But I can tell you I don't tell dirty jokes in a theatre. I like to get as close to the line as possible, maybe even cause a little embarrassment, but not hurt anybody, and I know how far I can go, I've learned through the years. As Dave Broadfoot says, 'I'm old enough to say what I want to say,' and Dave's right.

Dad didn't show a great affection, and never showed that he was proud of what I had achieved. About as close as he ever came . . . I remember one time I came home to London. I had a new Cadillac and he said, "Will you go to church with

32

Gordie Tapp

me Sunday morning?" I said, "Yes, I'll pick you up." I picked him up and I took him to church.

When we were coming out of the Baptist church my father said, "Reverend, I would like you to meet my son." I shook hands with the Reverend. "And that's his car over there." I thought then that my father was proud, but he certainly didn't want to tell me.

My dad was a lot different than his father, my grandfather. I remember my grandfather gave me this advice – 'do all you can when you are young . . . you will have lots of memories when you are old.' Isn't that marvelous? I have lived my life with grandfather's words ringing in my ears. You know, he was right.

Mom, on the other hand, was quite different with me than dad. Whenever we had company or family gatherings, she would ask me to get the guitar, and I'd have to sing songs like *The Burglar Under the Bed* and *Strawberry Roan*. Her favourite song was *Ramona*. I remember that we had the piano music for it. Mother played, but not that well, but she really loved that song.

Mom's twin sister, Olive, also played piano, but she always played hymns. Whenever she got going she used to drive us out of the house singing them.

That's about all I can tell you about mom. Well, I'll tell you one thing I do remember. It was Valentine's Day, and we lived I would say two-and-a-half or three miles from school. We lived on Chester Street and the school was on Brick Street. We called it Brick Street then, but it's Commissioners Road now.

We didn't have any money to buy Valentine cards, so I made up a bunch on the kitchen table. I just drew on some cardboard, I think it was the back of a Corn Flakes box. I took them out to put them in the box at school where all the kids placed their cards. About 11 o'clock in the morning there was a knock at the classroom door, somebody went to the door and said, "it's for Gordie Tapp."

I went to the door. It was my mother. She had found some old Valentine cards and scratched the names off them. I guess they were written in pencil. She gave them to me to write names on. I had to get to the box to see if I could find the old cardboard ones I had put in. I never forgot that, she found those and walked all the way to the school, so I wouldn't be disappointed or wouldn't feel badly that I had to give a Valentine card that I made myself. I guess that tells something about her character.

Gordie Tapp

Over the years cartoonists and caricaturists have loved to capture Gordie with their brilliant work. Never is their work flattering - it's not meant to be - but always Gordie has been flattered by them taking time to sketch him as they see him. Here they went for the barnyard feeling for the gang of *Country Hoedown*. With Gordie, they always picked on his nose.

Country Hoedown program for one of Gordie's tours.

Gordie Tapp

Gordie Tapp family photo

Gordie and Helen looking pretty dapper on a cruise boat in Italy when he entertained for Bob's Cruises of Oakville, Ontario.

4

'I can't be serious - we'd starve'

My biggest break in show business came when I was 20 years of age. I was in the Canadian Army, and they had an amateur contest. I was stationed in Debert, Nova Scotia. Of course, I had taken my guitar.

I'd sit up on the bunk at night and sing George Formby songs, crazy songs like *Mister Woo's A Window Cleaner, Leaning on a Lamp Post* and *The Burglar Under the Bed*. And I would imitate people that were popular on the radio back in those days, Amos and Andy, Donald Duck, Jimmy Fiddler, Kate Smith. Yeah, Kate Smith. All the guys said, 'why don't you go in that contest?' I said, 'Nah, I won't.' They said, 'go on.' So I said 'what the heck,' and I went over and applied, and won it. And the rest, as they say, is history.

They immediately put me as Master of Ceremonies for a show for the Canadian Legion. It was quite successful, so they moved me to Halifax and put me with a concert party. We worked all the armed forces bases in the area.

That's when I began to hone my craft. I began to store material mentally. I didn't have enough sense to write it down. Fortunately, I have the kind of mind that has maintained it. I can tell you jokes that Bob Hope told 50 years ago on radio, because I remember them. You can't suggest a subject that doesn't bring a joke to my mind. My wife often says, 'can't you be serious for a few minutes?' And I say, "I probably could, but we'd starve."

Gordie Tapp

Anyway, back to the army. I was placed as MC for B Company in an army show. We did the Laetitia, the Lady Nelson, they were hospital ships, and the

Gordie home on leave in London

Repats out of Hong Kong were all brought home on the Queen Mary. We entertained all of them. It began to become evident that I wanted to become an entertainer.

After we were married on January 3rd, 1944, Helen came down to Halifax and stayed with me. She got a job and worked while she was there. When I would entertain the ships coming in, she would come down with me. She happened to be there the very night her brother, John Mair, came home from overseas on the New Amsterdam. I'd made arrangements to get down close to the gangplank. They brought him out. He came down the gangplank and hugged her. Of course there were 2,000 men up on the decks cheering and hollering.

Those are the things that bring back a lot of memories.

When I was discharged from the armed forces I didn't know what I was going to do. Before the war I had worked at Scott McHale's shoe factory. I didn't even have my Grade 9 education, but I didn't want to go back to work there. My dad said that my job was waiting for me at the shoe factory. I said I didn't want to get dirty hands again. "Well, what are you going to do?" "I'm going to do something, but I'm not going to go back into the shoe factory."

I had recommendations for different things, I tried them, but I wasn't happy.

'I can't be serious - we'd starve'

My wife Helen worked at the department of Veterans Affairs. She asked one of the counselors how I could use the talents I had for entertaining. He suggested that I try the Lorne Greene Academy of Radio Arts, later called the Lorne Greene School of Home Economics by comedians Wayne and Shuster.

Gordie at CFGM Radio promoting *Country Hoedown*.

Gordie Tapp

Lorne Greene at the microphone at his Academy of Radio Arts in Toronto. Lorne was the voice of CBC News during World War II - and was known as 'The Voice of Doom' - before he became famous with another generation of Canadians as the star of television's western series, *Bonanza*.

Back to high school at age 23

Gordie reads a script at the radio academy with George Wilson, who went on to become a well-known classical music announcer in Canadian radio. In the back is Alfie Scopp, seated, who played the Hebrew reader in the movie *Fiddler on the Roof*.

5

Back to high school at age 23

So I had an interview with Lorne Greene and Lorne turned me down. He said, "You don't have enough education, I'm sorry." He was very nice about it. I went home very disappointed. My wife got together a scrapbook of all the things I had done while entertaining in the army, with pictures and write-ups and so on. They were quite flattering. This scrapbook became the first of many compiled by Helen.

I made another appointment, and Lorne reluctantly saw me. I presented the scrapbook and clippings to him and said, "Now here, I have this ability, what can I do?" He said, "There's only one way you can come into the academy, you have to go back to school and write your Senior Matriculation."

Well, that was a serious undertaking for a guy that was now 23 years of age. I really wanted to get into that radio arts academy. So the decision to get my education was a no-brainer.

Anyway, I went back to school, rehab school, it was in Kitchener, Ontario. I remember Howie Meeker, who went on to play in the National Hockey League with the Toronto Maple Leafs and then be a *Hockey Night In Canada* commentator, was in my Latin class. It's kind of interesting. When the school hired teachers, of course we made a lot of jokes. We said that they were so old that when they taught they used a chisel on the slate, but if you dropped your

Back to high school at age 23

pencil you missed two weeks of work, they really moved that fast. In fact, I wrote my Senior in less than six months. When I got that finished I started at the Academy in 1946 and graduated in 1947.

I was the first one hired out of our class, I got a job working at the brand-new Niagara Falls radio station. It was the first radio station in Niagara Falls and when I look back I think how amazing it was - and how fortunate I was - to be a pioneer in a new medium. In fact, I went down before it opened and was there for the official opening. I had a show called *What's on Tapp?* which ran from midnight until six in the morning. We changed that around after a while because it became a drag and there weren't enough sponsors through the night. So we finished up at 12:30 at night. I went from 10:30 to 12:30.

Then I got a chance to go to Guelph. I was making $35 a week in Niagara Falls, and I went up to Guelph for $40, I think it was.

I got a job working in a nightclub called the Paradise Gardens for which I picked up another $15. Things had begun to happen for me.

Then I was hired to go to CHML in Hamilton for $55 a week. I sold my own time in five-minute segments for *What's on Tapp?* and I can remember my first paycheque was $85. I was quite thrilled. I remember walking to the bank thinking 'I wonder if they have enough money to cash this?' I was a real rube.

Lorne Greene's Academy of Radio Arts was on Jarvis Street, right across from the CBC. In fact, we took a lot of our classes right in the CBC studios. We had teachers from the CBC like Andrew Allen, Lister Sinclair, Mavor Moore, and the director of speech for the CBC at that time Mr. Brodie. I can remember him telling us there was no G in luxury, and the word was Extraordinary, not Extra-Ordinary. Those are the things that stay in your mind. The course was very good. We had acting classes, took writing courses, and we learned about sound effects, which was taught by Sid Lancaster, who was the head sound effects man at the CBC.

Even Jack Kent Cooke, who started with Roy Thomson in radio and newspapers in Northern Ontario and went on to own NFL and NBA teams, came and gave us lectures on several different things, principally operating a radio station. Of course, the emphasis was on radio, because TV had not come along at that time.

Leslie Nielsen was one of our classmates. He went on to become the famous

Gordie Tapp

Gordie and Leslie Nielsen share a laugh at the Foster Brooks golf tournament in Louisville, Kentucky, long after they had both graduated from Lorne Greene's Academy of Radio Arts.

Leslie Nielsen of Hollywood movie fame. One time at the academy he had a hot date. He was going to take Miss Canadian Radio to the Canadian Radio Ball, and I was working extra little ditties here and there, conventions and so on, making an extra $15 or $20 a week. It afforded me a few things I couldn't have on the money I was getting to go to college.

Anyway, I had bought a Chesterfield coat, a beautiful black coat with a velvet collar. Leslie was going to take this young lady to the ball, and he asked me if he could borrow the coat, and I said, "sure," so I lent it to him.

That evening I got a telephone call from Alex Bedard, another of our classmates, who said, "I don't know if you know it or not, Gordie, but Clarence Mack was mad because Les took the young lady to the ball, and he's waiting at his apartment with a gun. Now Les is wearing your coat, and if he shoots him, the coat's going to have a hole in it." I immediately rushed out to meet Les before he got home, before Mack shot him. But it didn't happen, I got my coat back and it didn't have any holes in it.

We were young and we were crazy. I had that Chesterfield coat and Homburg hat, and we would go down to the Royal Alex Theatre. I would stand in front of about a half-dozen of the students including Len Starmer, who became the Executive Producer for the CBC on all the variety shows. They used to say, "Oh there he is," and come and ask me for an autograph. Soon I'd have a whole crowd of people around me and I'd just sign anything, and they'd go away and think, "Who is he? He must be famous because everyone wants his autograph."

We used to go up to the Midtown theatre, it was below Bloor on the west side of Yonge Street in downtown Toronto. The had a long stairs, and we used to play 'Bank Robber' and shoot each other and roll down those damn stairs right to the bottom until the management would come and kick us out. I guess it was all part of our learning experience.

Four or five of us would walk into the Eaton's store on Yonge Street and head for the clock department, where there were 450 clocks. We'd draw straws on who'd have to go and ask the girl the time.

George Wilson, who later became very famous as a classical music announcer with CFRB, was with us at the academy. He was best known as Crazy George, and when we'd take the streetcar up Yonge Street, George would run beside us. He'd rest when we got to Wellesley and Bloor streets, while the streetcar was stopped.

Another thing he used to do when we'd get on the streetcar is stay at the front, while we would go to the back and sit down. Then when the streetcar got crowded, he'd start his trek through all the people, working his way towards the back of the streetcar where we were seated. "Excuse me. Pardon me," and he'd shuffle along the aisle until he got to us. We'd be all crying with laughter in the back.

Funny thing was we were grown men - all discharged from the Army. I guess it was play acting, and that was what we were all working towards. That was to be our vocation in life and we practiced it on the public. It was all innocent fun. Didn't harm anyone.

You never wanted to miss Lister Sinclair's classes because you never actually knew what Lister was going to say. We were studying writing for radio, and he had as an example a play he had written called *Out of Darkness*. It was about cancer, and back in those days, the way people looked at it, the chance for a

Gordie Tapp

Gordie's graduation certificate from Lorne Greene's Academy of Radio Arts in 1947.

cure was becoming greater each year.

He taught us how to write about serious things that would make people take notice and probably change their way of life to avoid this sort of thing. He talked about cancer of the cervix. One of the students, I can remember his name, but I won't mention it, put up his hand and said, "Sir, what is the cervix?" Lister Sinclair, in his own inimitable way, reached into a cone of French fries that he kept in the inkwell on the front of his desk, took out two and he stuffed them in his mouth and pushed them in with two fingers, chewed them slowly, and looked over the class and said, "The cervix is part of the womb, so obviously it concerns a very small percentage of the class." We all laughed because there were only a few girls sitting in the class. But it was beautiful the way he did it. He could have answered it in many ways, but he answered it in Lister Sinclair's way. He was a great instructor, and is still a great man, and we still hear him on the radio and admire him.

Another name comes to mind. Jimmy Doonin was the year before us at the academy, but went to Hollywood and played Scotty on Star Trek for a thousand

45

years. He's passed on out there and so has John Vernon, another well-known Canadian actor to make it in Hollywood. There were a lot of people in our class. I think about 85 per cent went into the entertainment business in various roles - operating radio stations as far west as Victoria and getting prominent positions in the Prairies, besides all those who went to Hollywood. It's very interesting to see the different routes the fellows followed. I look back and see what a great group of people I was privileged to study with at the academy.

Gordie's 1947 graduation class at the Lorne Greene Academy of Radio Arts. Lorne Greene is on the right about half-way up with his face partially cut off. Gordie is on the left of the three students at the top of the picture.

Gordie Tapp family photo

6

'Greatest experience' entering radio academy

After the war when I had to go back to school to get enough education to enter the Academy of Radio Arts, I consider that was the greatest experience in my life. I've mentioned some of the people who were in my class. Others were:

- Teddy Forman, who became Miss Teddy on CBC television.

- Drew Crossen, who went on to be one of the prominent producers in the country, producing *Country Hoedown* at one time.

- Fred Davis, who we all know from *Front Page Challenge*, one of the most recognizable figures on Canadian television for many years.

- Alfie Scopp, a TV and radio performer in Canada, who made several movies, including *Fiddler on the Roof*. He played a very prominent part.

- Len Starmer who became Executive Producer for light entertainment for the CBC.

- Tom Harvey, well known television and motion picture actor. He's still working.

- George Wilson, who was very well known in radio and who was with CFRB for years and years.

'Greatest experience' entering radio academy

It's wonderful to have had the experience of entertaining and working with these guys, all great talents in their own field.

Just before Lorne Greene passed away we had a reunion, and it worked out so wonderfully well. The guys responsible for it did a great job of bringing it together. I was lucky enough to be Master of Ceremonies. I rode in on a little buckskin horse, the same colour of horse that Lorne rode in the *Bonanza* series. He got quite the kick out of that.

I have several pictures of me climbing down off the horse and saluting him when we rode in, to the theme of *Bonanza*, played by the band. This was at the Royal York Hotel in downtown Toronto and you should have seen the faces of the hotel guests and staff when I rode into the hotel on the horse and then took the elevator to Lorne's event. It's not every day that a horse gets on an elevator in a top class hotel.

I am sure you are wondering whether the horse left any presents in the hotel. Well, we took precautions to prevent any accidents happening by having the horse raked. Yes, a lot of wonderful experiences, a lot of wonderful stories, a lot of wonderful memories.

Gordie in his early days in radio.

I was always an entertainer, even when I was a kid at school. Besides playing the harmonica and guitar and entertaining at garden parties and functions like that, I think probably when I won the amateur contest in Debert, Nova Scotia, put on by the Canadian Legion, I then went to Halifax and joined the concert party and started entertaining around Halifax. That was a major turning point in my life.

48

Gordie Tapp

It gave me the feeling that I wanted to entertain and not return to the factory.

It was a turning point in my life that really was important, I understood what I wanted for the first time in my life, I wasn't wandering around wondering what I wanted to be and what I wanted to do, so I aimed in that direction. Being accepted in the Academy of Radio Arts was another big thing for me. I admired the business and wanted to be in it.

I knew I didn't have the education, but I gained that with hard work and effort and then the Academy gave me the opportunity to display my talents and really focus on what I wanted to do. Lorne was right to insist that I get a proper education.

Gordie in his Guelph days

Could I have done what I have done in the entertainment field without my high school? Probably. But it would have been hard. I needed that little extra. It gave me the confidence to know that I could do it. It gave me that little extra polish that stood me in good stead when I interviewed, mixed and mingled with numerous newsmakers, politicians, entertainers, sports figures, even world leaders.

When I was at my first radio station CHVC Niagara Falls, I had the opportunity to go to WKBW in Buffalo. Foster Brooks was over in Buffalo and I used to do a Saturday night record hop in Niagara Falls, New York. That's where I first had the chance to meet him. I had the opportunity to go to Buffalo to work, but I turned it down. It was difficult for me to do that at the time, but probably it was one of the best things I did.

Gordie in the early years in radio.

It would have been nice to move to the United States and start to work in the fledgling radio business, but I stayed in Canada and eventually got the *Main Street Jamboree* going in Hamilton, which lead to *Country Hoedown*, and from that to *Hee Haw.*

Another turning point in my life was *Hee Haw*, when I eventually went to work in the United States. I was able to learn the advantages of working in

'Greatest experience' entering radio academy

America, thanks to the CBC. The training they gave me at the CBC meant I was able to go there and operate as if I knew what I was doing.

You have several turning points in your life, and I guess they're all important to you, as long as you do the things that you want to do.

I can't imagine what it would be like to work in a factory where you do the same thing day in and day out, not having an audience that you could thrill and make laugh and change their moods.

One thing that I must bring out at this time is the influence of my father's overly strict and the almost cloistered church life and that I lived, was very good training. It stood me in good stead, because the entertainment field where I worked was a business that was riddled with difficulties, especially if you let them get a hold of you.

There was booze, of course, and drugs, and some of my friends were using them, and saying, "Come on, have one." I'd say "No," and they'd say, "There's the preacher." I guess it was good to be called the preacher, I'd go back to my room and think, 'Dad wouldn't have liked that if I'd done that.' It really helped me.

I always liked beautiful women, but I guess I'm no different from any other man in that respect. However, I worked with some of the most beautiful women in the business. I guess it would have been easy enough to run away and have a good time and think everything was wonderful. But then I thought about my good wife and my upbringing, which was strict enough to make me realize that those kind of difficulties exist, and you make them for yourself if you yield to the temptation. I thanked my father many times for my training, even though when I was a young buck I used to think, "Gosh, how can he be so strict? Why do I have to do everything he says?" But I guess it's paid off.

Freddie Morgan, who was one of the Spike Jones band members, did a comedy sketch dressed like Stalin. He had a picture of him doing the skit and I said I'd like a copy of the picture. He gave it to me and autographed it.

I carried it around with me for a while. One day I crossed over the border into the United States to sell time on my radio show in Niagara Falls, Ontario. I had several sponsors in Niagara Falls, New York.

Returning to Canada, most of the guys knew me on the bridge and it was, "Hi Gordie, there you go." This day they had a new guy on duty, and he said, "What's in the case?" I said, "Oh, just papers from my sales."

50

Gordie Tapp

It's not who you think it is . . . or who Canada Customs at Niagara Falls thought it was when they found this autographed 'Stalin' picture in Gordie's briefcase.

He said, "we'd better take a look at them." He looks in it and pulls out this picture of Stalin, which is written in Russian on the bottom and signed 'Joe Stalin.' I said, "That's one of the guys in the Spike Jones band." He said, "Oh is that so? You'd better come into this room."

He left the room and went and got two other guys. They were asking me all kinds of questions. I said, "I don't know what you guys are talking about, that's just a picture of a friend of mine."

Well I was there for an hour arguing with them when finally one of the guys came in and said, "Hi Gordie." "Oh, do you know him?" He said, "Yeah, he's a disc jockey at the radio station across the bridge." They said, "Well, look at this. Who is it Gordie?" I said "It's Freddie Morgan from the Spike Jones band." He said, "I've seen him do that on stage, they were here not that long ago." The guy said, "Ok, you can go Tapp." It's funny the way things happen, I've had that picture for a lot of years.

51

Gordie interviews Martha Raye, one of the many world entertainment stars who used to play Burlington's Brant Inn, owned by Murray Anderson, centre.

7

Gordie didn't want to do Country

It was Tom Darling who introduced me to country music at CHML in Hamilton. I didn't want any part of it, because I was playing Stan Kenton and Boyd Raeburn and that kind of music. I loved the big band sound.

Tom wanted me to do a country music show, which I was not particularly fond of doing. So he said, "Do it for a couple of weeks, we'll see how it works."

Well it worked out fine and he asked me to stay, I said, "I can't, I don't want to." He said, "Look, I'll give you another $35 a week." Well, back in those days another $35 was pretty darn nice.

So I ended up making pretty good money back in those days. Some weeks I was making over $350 a week, which was a lot of money. We bought a house. The country music show that we started was called the *Main Street Jamboree* which was sponsored by 7-up and Success Wax.

We went to network radio on the CBC and then when television came along we went to Channel 11, starting at 7 o'clock on Saturday night. It ran after I left it in 1956 to host a country music show called *Country Hoedown* on CBC. Funny, Tommy Hunter came to us and worked with us on the old *Main Street Jamboree*. When I went over, Tommy was auditioning to work on *Country Hoedown*, and he became a regular cast member.

Gordie didn't want to do Country

Gordie, Tommy Hunter and The Hames Sisters ready for a trip to entertain Canadian troops.

Of course, you know the success of that show on Saturday night prior to the hockey games. Tommy stayed with the show, and when I left it became the

Tommy Hunter Show. He stayed on air for 30 years. He had quite a record on television.

Up until 1967 I had a radio show on the CBC in the morning before it was dropped, but during that period I did several other television shows, one called *Front and Centre*, which was done by Saul Ilson who went on to Hollywood fame and I did a TV show with Tony Orlando and Saul produced it. I also did a show called *PM Party,* which featured Alan Blye, who went to Hollywood and became a famous director. In 1969 it was my turn to go to Hollywood to start *Hee Haw.*

Gordie with Hank Snow.

Gordie Tapp

The Country Hoedown cast belts out a number. Gordie is leaning on the piano, second from the left, back row. Gordon Lightfoot, then a member of the Singing Swinging Eight is third from the right..

Gordie on a TV show with Wally Koster.

Gordie pays stripper $50
to scare pants off Tommy

Country Hoedown lasted some nine-and-a-half-years, from 1956 to 1965, then we had a half season as a summer replacement. Some wonderful people were on the show, including Tommy Common, who had a terrific voice.

Tommy was not a big man, but a very difficult man to know. If you said to Tommy, "What are you going to do this weekend?" He'd say, "I'm going up North." You'd say, "Where up North?" "Up North."

He never really did let you see inside him, not like some people. I was very close with Maurice Boyler, who was on the show, playing banjo.

Al Cherney, a dear, dear wonderful guy, travelled with me all over the world. In fact, Al was Ukrainian and I used to kid him and call him the Russian. He'd come in late at night, when we were overseas, and he'd turn out the light, take off his clothes, cover me up and kiss me on the forehead. I appreciated that because I knew that Al was just a real, wonderful, warm man. Don't read anything into that about Al or myself. It's not uncommon in Russia, because the men kiss each other.

Tommy Common was a bit of a disturber, he loved to cause problems. He got me into some pretty sticky positions, some things that I'd love to be able to

Gordie pays stripper $50 to scare pants off Tommy

Tommy Common, The Hames Sisters and Tommy Hunter back up Cousin Clem on *Country Hoedown*.

tell you about. I had claustrophobia, and we were doing a number called *Old Joe Clarke*. It was set in a scene in front of a small, old railroad station. We had a huge wicker trunk that was lined in plastic. I had to get into the trunk while Tommy sang the first verse of the song, then he would jump off and

Gordie Tapp

Gordie with The Hames Sisters at a dress rehearsal.

open the trunk and I would get out and we'd do a couple of verses together, and then the dancers would come in, and we'd close the number. He knew I had claustrophobia, and damned if he didn't tie me in that trunk. He tied it so I couldn't get out. I nearly went frantic, and when I finally got out of there I thought, "I've got to teach you a lesson, young man."

His manager was Ian Reid. I called Ian and said, "I want to do something to Tommy on the dress rehearsal, and I want to scare the wits off him."

"What did you have in mind?"

"I want a stripper. If you can get me a stripper, I'll pay her." It cost me $50. We brought her down from the Gaiety in Toronto, and she came with nothing on but a fur coat. We put her in that trunk for the dress rehearsal. The music starts,

Gordie pays stripper $50 to scare pants off Tommy

Gordie with Charlie Chamberlain, a favourite for many years with the Don Messer Show.

Tommy jumps on the trunk and says, "is he in here?" and then he laughs all over, and did the first verse. Of course, everyone was in on it except Tom. When he finished singing the first verse, he jumped off the trunk, lifted the hood, all the lights went off, then the spotlight hit the trunk and the band played da-da-da-da-da, da-da-da-da-da-da-da, you know, the *Hoochie Coochie* and that girl came squirming out. I've never seen anyone so frightened in my life.

CBC Still Photo Collection

Pat Hervey with Gordie on *Country Hoedown*.

Tommy said later, "You know guys, I took hold of that ladder and got a message from the spirit world." That really moved him, he was always playing tricks.

We had some wonderful things happen on *Country Hoedown*, I had a little Tamworth pig, and I used him on the show. I put a little red bow on his neck, and he'd run around with me on the set. I had a little forked stick, and I used to control him with that, trying to keep him in line, because he wanted to run all over the place.

I was working with him one night, and he got to squealing. Of course that raised the ire of every animal lover and they telephoned the CBC and claimed, "He's hurting that pig." Little do they know, it's pretty hard to hurt a pig. They're pretty strong and they have their own mind.

GORDIE

A man of many voices **and** *characters!*

CBC Still Photo Collection

I don't usually wear feathers . . .

It looks like Gordie was let loose in the costume department at CBC in Toronto. Gordie does not remember why he was in the getups on the following pages . . .

Anyway, this little pig was agitated because I was trying to make him do something he didn't want to do. He relieved himself right on the floor, an accident I'm sure. I swung the stick around and it hit the manure, and it flew and hit the band. You could see the band jumping and trying to duck.

After the show the producer had us all together, and our orchestra leader, who shall remain nameless, complained bitterly to the producer that he and the band were covered in manure. "No wonder," I said, "You played like an A.H. all night." It didn't go over too well with the band, but everyone else laughed.

Lorraine Forman was the first female solo performer on *Country Hoedown* and it was no surprise that she went on and did so well in Hollywood and on Broadway.

Later, Pat Hervey was a very pleasant addition to our cast.

Country Hoedown was a very well rehearsed show. It was at the beginning of television. We went on the air in 1956, and television had started in Canada in 1953.

Gordie Tapp

Do I look like Elton John?

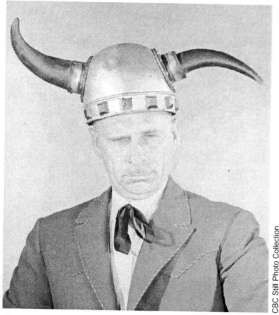

No horny jokes, please . . .

We would rehearse Tuesday and Thursday. Friday morning we'd do the dress rehearsal, Friday afternoon we'd do a cleanup, Friday night we did the show live.

Live television is different than taped television because in a taped show you knew you could correct the situation. When we did it live, you knew that if the door didn't open, it wasn't going to open, and so you had to ad-lib your way around it. We had to ad-lib on many occasions. Two guys pulling ropes could hoist someone up, and if the ropes didn't work you'd have to have an ad-lib ready or it had to wait to be done on the next show because it didn't work on this one. It was a whole different way of television.

Tommy Common, a great little artist, great little performer. He'd work those songs over, never needed a retake, I was amazed.

Tommy Hunter was the same. These guys were pros, and they worked hard, and made it look real for the audience. I guess that's what made the whole show - everybody's dedication to making it something that people could enjoy.

Country Hoedown was done in Toronto and telling these stories reminds me

Gordie pays stripper $50 to scare pants off Tommy

Who put the lights out?

Ah, that's a little bit better . . .

of the one about the guy who came up from the States. A cab driver was driving him around, he said, "Ahh, the buildings in Dallas are taller than this.' Everything appeared to be bigger and better in Texas. Then he saw one place and said, "that's a bit of an interesting building." The driver said, "oh my gosh, when I came by here the other day they were just putting in the foundations. And look at that, there's a sign that they're kicking people out that haven't paid their rent. They move fast."

I tell another story of a Texan who came up to Toronto, and said everything was "bigger in Texas, better in Texas, taller in Texas." The guys got sick of listening to this so they got him drunk and took him to the cemetery and sat him up against a gravestone then stood back to watch what would happen when he woke up. Well, he slept the whole night and in the morning he woke up, looked around and said, "Well look at that, the Resurrection Morning and the Texan is the first one up."

Gordie Tapp

Hair today . . .   . . . gone tomorrow.

Texas really is quite a state, but I always used to tell my audiences, "Canada is really big, you can put all of the United States, including Texas and Alaska - and Texas and Alaska a second time - into Canada," and they look at you like you're nuts. But Canada's that big.

65

Tommy Common always the joker

Gordie, in his Cousin Clem gear, with Tommy Common and Grandpa Jones.

9

Tommy Common
always the joker

Going back to *Country Hoedown* days, Tommy Common never did anything mean, but he was a trickster.

We had a party in Saskatoon, or maybe it was Regina. Either way, we were doing the grandstand show, and we were staying at a local hotel.

We had a party that night, some of the people from the show, entertainers and crew together.

I came down to my room at probably quarter to 12 at night and I went in and there was a blonde girl in my bed. She was obviously inebriated and had no clothes on. Not wanting to have any problems, I went back to the party and got one of the fellows I knew to help me get her dressed, and take her to a room on the main floor where the staff would go and hang their clothes and comb their hair and so on.

We took her in there and put her on a couch, and left her. I went to bed that night, and then I thought, how on earth would that girl get in my room? So I got up and went downstairs and talked to the clerk and asked if anyone had got the key to my room. He said, 'oh yes, Mr. Common got the key, because he said he had some music to put in your room.' So I thought, oh well, I'll see him in the morning. So I went to bed.

Tommy Common always the joker

Next morning, I see Tommy sitting with two policemen. Tom says, 'he was with her the last I saw her.'

I went over to them and said, 'what's the problem fellows?' They said, 'we're looking for a missing person.' I said, 'I think I know where we can find her.' One of the policemen said, 'I hope so, Mr. Tapp, because it looks kind of bad.'

Anyway I took him into the room where the staff combed their hair and hung their clothes, and there she was fast asleep on the couch. The policemen said, 'thank you very much,' and took her, and that was the end of that.

Tommy just sat there with that silly smirk on his face, I'll never forget it. He really knew how to cause problems.

Another time I had a problem like that, I don't think I was doing *Hee Haw* at the time, so it must have been 1968. I went to Saskatoon to entertain at the Sportswomen's Banquet, where they gave out awards to all the sportswomen who had won contests across Saskatchewan.

After the show, I stayed to sign autographs and talk to people. One of the guys from the show came up to me and said, "Give me the key to your room, will you?" I said, "What's going on?"

'Well, your room is a suite, and we need a suite, we're all going to go up there.'

When I finished up signing and talking, about an hour later, I went up to the room. It was full of people, I mean they were everywhere. They were having beer. They were having drinks. They were having one heck of a time. Music was blaring and some were dancing.

I put up with that for about an hour, then I said, 'I've had enough of it, I want everybody to go, let's go. I've got to leave in the morning, so let's get going.' I won't mention any names, except for Spike, who was the sports announcer.

Anyway, they all cleared out of the room, and I closed the door and went into my bedroom and there was a girl in my bed. 'Holy smokes,' I said, I don't need this, what's going on? She was obviously three sheets to the wind.

She did have her clothes on. I managed to get her up and get her sorted out, and I asked her if she knew where she lived. She said 'yes,' and I said, 'come on, I'm going to take you home.' She says, 'you don't have to take me home, I have my own car.' I said, 'well, that's fine, come on I'll take you down to the car.'

So I took her downstairs, through the lobby, and people were looking at us when we walked through the hotel. Her hair was all askew, and clothes all ruffled up. Anyway, we get to her car, and I said, 'give me your keys.' She said, 'oh no, I'm going to drive.' I said, 'you're in no shape to drive.' She said, 'if I go, I'm going to drive.' So I said, 'alright, you get in and I'll get in with you.'

So I did, and we started out. We went about two blocks from the hotel and she was all over the road. I reached over and grabbed the keys and said, 'look, you are in no shape to drive, I'm going to take these keys.' She said, 'don't you touch them.' I said, 'ok, stop the car.' She stopped. I got out and closed the door,. She took off and I walked back to the hotel.

The next morning, about 6:30 I get a call. It's Spike. I said, "What do you want?" He said, "What did you do, get out and run? I said, "I don't know what you're talking about." He says, "The broad we put in your bed . . . were you in the car with her?' I said, "Yeah, but she went two blocks from here and I noticed she couldn't drive properly, and I told her if she didn't let me drive, she'd have to let me out. I got out and walked back."'

He said, 'boy, you're lucky. She sideswiped a car, hit a pole, and she's in the hospital under police guard.'

I said, 'whoa Spike, once again you guys came close to causing unnecessary embarrassment. You know, I can just see the headlines, "CBC employee caught with drunken women," and how do you explain that sort of thing to your wife?

Once again, I think the man upstairs was looking out for me. That wasn't a Tommy Common prank, but that was the kind of joke he used to play.

'Tying one on' with Al Cherney

Gordie and Al Cherney were the best of friends.

10

'Tying one on' with Al Cherney

Fiddle player Al Cherney was a dear friend. His real name was Alex Ciernevic. He was Ukrainian and he talked to me in Ukrainian all the time. In fact, I learned quite a bit. When we lost Al very young in life, I did part of his eulogy in Ukrainian and got introduced to the language with everybody coming up and trying to talk to me after thinking I was fully knowledgeable in the language. I am not.

Al and I had a fabulous relationship as you will see from this story. We were on tour with the *Country Hoedown* show and we were in Swift Current, Saskatchewan. There was Al Cherney, The Hames Sisters, Tommy Common and myself. We had a pickup band that we got out of Calgary.

We were leaving Swift Current about midnight, after the show and I had pretty close to $5,000 in cash that they'd paid me for the show. While that was a good price in those days, it would not be acceptable today.

Alex was driving me and The Hames Sisters were with Tommy Common, and as we were driving, Al says, 'there's a car following us.' I said, 'I wonder if they know we've got this money, what do we have in this car for protection?' He said, 'there's a tire iron in the back seat,' so I got in the back and got the tire iron and got up front and sat with him. I said, 'OK, slow down and pull

'Tying one on' with Al Cherney

over and let's see what he wants.' We stopped and the guy pulled up in front of us and got out and came back with a little silver box about a foot long and about four inches wide. He said, 'one of you boys left your tie in the dressing room.' We thanked him very much. I looked at Al and he looked at me and I said, 'I didn't leave a tie.' He said, "neither did I."

Al Cherney

We started to drive, and we opened the box and in it was the worst looking tie you've ever seen in your life. It was about an inch-and-a-half wide, and it was brown and green and it was just . . . well, words can't describe it. Let's just say we wouldn't wear that kind of tie.

Well, when we got back home, I had the tie, and I drove Al to the airport. He was flying to Montreal to do a command performance for Prince Philip. Al was a great fiddler, one of the best. I worked with all the best in Nashville and I tell you, none of them could hold a candle to this guy. He was trained as a classical musician and he used all his abilities as a classical musician to create country music, and he made it sound so great.

Anyway, I went with him to the airport and when he was getting his ticket I opened his fiddle case and I tied the tie around the neck of his fiddle. When he got to Montreal he opened it up and broke up laughing. He thought it was very funny.

That Christmas I got the tie back. He gave it to me with a pair of brown socks. The following Christmas I took it with me to Cyprus, because I was working there and I mailed it from Cyprus to Al for a Christmas present with a card. He was taking his son Peter to hockey practice, and he said, 'I'd better stop at the

Gordie Tapp

Cousin Clem leads the *Country Hoedown* regulars, including Tommy Hunter, right, and Al Cherney, left.

Post Office, there's a package there for me.'

He stood in line for half-an-hour in the Christmas rush, and when he finally got to the counter the postal worker handed him a box and he looked at it and said, 'it's that damned tie!' He knew just by looking at the box and who it was from. We laughed about that.

On my birthday he gave the tie back to me with a pair of green suspenders. Come his birthday, Helen, my wife, was doing cake decorations and she took the cover of his album and did a picture on the top of the cake of Al playing the fiddle. It was beautifully done. She baked the tie inside the cake.

They had company when they were cutting into the cake. They found the tie and thought that it was crazy.

The next time I got it back I was ploughing at the farm and this plane kept zooming overhead. I knew Maurice Bolyer had a plane, and I thought, "that's

'Tying one on' with Al Cherney

Johnny Cash started it off with his concerts at Folsom Prison and San Quentin. Gordie entertained at Maplehurst Correctional Centre in Milton, with Al Cherney and folk singer John Allan Cameron. With them is Marie Gies, a secretary at the centre. At a prison concert in Prince Albert, Saskatchewan, Gordie says he just wasn't thinking when he sang the ballad *Please Release Me Let Me Go.*

gotta be Maurice," for some reason. Well, they dropped the tie out with a little parachute and it came down and landed in the field and I retrieved it.

Come Christmas I gave Al bottle of Vermouth. He liked Vermouth. I made a wire rack bracket to put the tie down in the bottle. I steamed the top off the bottle, put the tie in and steamed the top back on again. It was perfect. You couldn't tell that the top had been tampered with.

Al tells the story . . . it was in April and the bottle was sitting on his mantle. Somebody visiting him said, "there's something in that bottle." Al said, "I know, it's Vermouth, Gordie gave it to me for Christmas."

"No no, I mean there's something in the bottle."

Al looked at him and said, "I bet it's that bloody tie!" He opened it up and took the tie out and got a pretty good kick out of it.

On my birthday he gave it to me with a brown country shirt, very distasteful, but a good gag. For his birthday I had my picture taken in the nude, holding my privates, wearing only the tie. To be kind of ridiculous I got the photograph blown up to 8 x 10 and signed it in Ukrainian, Moy Melenke and Happy Birthday and sent it to him. But I kept the tie.

Later on that year we were doing *Hee Haw* in Nashville and I was in the scene called Empty Arms Hotel where Roy Clark was the clerk and I walked on the set and rang the bell on the desk and Roy jumped up and said, "Empty Arms Hotel, oh it's you Mr. Gordon, I have something for you," and he held up this picture of me in the nude, wearing just the tie. Cherney had given it to him in Toronto when Roy played the *Tommy Hunter Show*. Of course, Roy held while all the cameras hit it and 20 monitors around TNN had my picture in the nude with this tie on. Of course, everyone got a great laugh, and thought it was marvelous.

Not long after that, it was the first of August, I got a call from Al and he said, "Gordie, I'm in the hospital and I've got what my father had." Well, I knew his dad died from bronchial cancer. I said, "Ok Al, I'll come and see you." He said, "no, don't come to see me, I don't want to see anyone." That was the first of August. We buried him on the third of September. It was that quick.

At the funeral we were standing by the coffin and his wife Merny was there. I said, "Merny, do you mind if I put the tie in the coffin?"

She said, "no, I don't mind, I think it belongs there."

So it's resting with Al wherever he is. He's got the tie. It was a lot of laughs and a lot of fun and a story that I've told many, many times.

Gordie Tapp

Gordie and Grandpa Jones kept everyone laughing with their antics in the General Store.

11

Entertaining Canadian troops all over the world

One thing that I am proud of doing was touring all over Canada and overseas to play shows for servicemen stationed abroad.

We did 27 tours for diplomatic corps and I must tell you an interesting sidelight in this respect.

When I first went to *Hee Haw* Grandpa Jones invited me out to his home. It had a beautiful plaque on the wall, all embossed in gold and signed by President Eisenhower. I said, "What did you get that for Pa?" He said, "I went to Korea." I said, "How often?" He said, "Once." I said, "Doing what?" He said, "Entertaining."

I started to laugh.

He said, "You don't believe me?" I said, "Yes, I believe you, but I did 27 tours around the world for Canadian Forces and never got a postcard from the Prime Minister."

I'm sure you'll find that with every Canadian show business personality because Canadians treat Canadians that way. We are not like the United States in that respect, and that's one thing I regret about us, but, there are a lot of things that I am in favour of over and above the way they do things in the U.S. I guess there's a lot more patriotism in the States - you're brought up

Entertaining troops all over the world

in your hometown, and you're loyal to your ways and your people and your customs. Whereas in Canada there is not an expectation that you would be loyal or patriotic. Let me put it another way - if you are born in Italy (or any other country for that matter) and move to the United States you become an American. If you were born in Italy and emigrate to Canada and take out your Canadian citizenship - and live here until your dying day - you are an Italo-Canadian. Who's right? Who's wrong? What is the best way? I don't know. I am sure they both have their pluses and minuses. I am getting into an area here where it gets very personal for everyone. Let me just say that I was born in Canada and will always be a Canadian. I love the country. It has been good to me and to my family.

I have worked in the United States and owned property there. Again, a marvellous country and one that has offered me and my family wonderful opportunities. But I have never had a desire to become an American. I am proud of my Canadian citizenship.

During the war, you'd see the American sailors and they'd have 24 ribbons on their chest. I'd always say to our Canadian sailors, "why aren't you guys like that?" And they'd say, "Hell, they get a ribbon for going to the bathroom!"

They reward theirs and we don't reward ours. It's just our way. We are not as demonstrative as our American friends. We just don't make a big deal out of anything, whereas the Americans make a big deal out of everything.

Have you ever seen a Canadian hold his hand or hat over his heart during the singing of the national anthem, O Canada? I haven't.

The letter from the President of the United States to an entertainer who devoted some time to entertain U.S. troops abroad is just one example of this. Mind you, I can't complain, my country has now rewarded me well enough, giving me the Order of Canada, the highest award offered by Canada. I guess you can't beat that.

Let me just say one more thing about this disparity in the way we both honour our citizens who go the extra mile. In some ways I like the American way because it honours the actions of someone while they are fresh in everyone's mind. They are spontaneous, but genuine. In Canada, however, we don't recognize the spontaneity of anything, the sprint to get something done when it is needed - and while it is happening - such as Grandpa Jones' one trip to entertain the U.S. troops.

In Canada you don't get any kudos for a sprint, unless you are known for being

Gordie Tapp

Cousin Clem entertaining troops in Camp Rafa, near Gaza.

the fastest man on earth, like Donovan Bailey or Ben Johnson. You've got to sustain things. It's almost like a marathon. It's a commitment of a lifetime, rather than a commitment of time.

When you allow time to creep between the deed and the reward - and please understand that we don't do things for rewards - the circumstances can change memories. In my case you'll see in a letter to me from the Prime Minister of Canada where he thanks me for 30 tours I made to entertain Canadian troops. Now I have always thought it was 27 tours. It's not a big deal for sure, but you can see how time has a habit of tainting the facts.

The main thing, as far as I am concerned, is that we were appreciated by the troops and their leaders whenever we went to perform at their base, whether it was here in Canada, up in the Arctic, or in Europe.

I particularly liked the following letter I received. We did those shows for the men and women who were standing on guard for us. It always made me feel good about being an entertainer for the troops. I came across this letter and I thought it might be interesting to read it. It says:

Entertaining troops all over the world

Gordie rode the tank back down from St.. Hilarian Castle, seen in the background, after refusing to ride the bus. Greeks looked after the bottom half of the mountain and Turkish troops guarded the top. When the Greek driver handed over the bus to the Turkish driver the new driver had problems getting the bus in gear on the side of the mountain. Trombonist Teddy Roderman, always the joker, said "look at all the old buses down there," pointing to the sheer drop. There were no wrecked buses, but Gordie didn't want to take any chances. The plains behind Gordie are where Richard The Lionheart jousted during the Crusades.

Canadian Army Contingent CFB05049 UNEF Middle East.

To: Gordie Tapp Esquire,

Dear Gordie,

I would be remiss if I did not drop you a line to say how much I enjoyed our association during your stay here. Seldom have I been so confident that a person would say or do the right thing at the right time, and you never disappointed me, either on the stage or at many of the social functions you attended. Although I had seen the program four times, the Canada Day performance gave me a special lift. The show was pertinent to the day and the show moved along under your expert control with zip and precision. All in all it was an outstanding two weeks which I thought ended with a nice climax. I hope you had a nice journey home and I wish you all the best in your TV roles.

Yours Sincerely,

D.W. Cunningham, Commander of the Canadian Contingent

And it's signed Doug.

Gordie Tapp

I have a marvelous memory for things, especially humour. I can remember jokes that people told me 50 years ago, and I can remember the name of the people who told it to me, which is something. I don't know what it means, but it's certainly been helpful to me.

When we entertained, let us say, the repats out of Hong Kong on the Queen Mary near the end of the war, I met a lot of senior officers who really had been through hell. Men that weighed 250 pounds were down to 130 because they had dysentery, beriberi or malaria and all kinds of other things that you get when you're not properly fed and don't get the right nutrition.

I can remember the stories, they're classic stories really, whether they'd mean anything in the book without an English accent, you decide:

Stories that went like this:

- Two kids went to Eton together in England, and they were very good friends. One day, on the cricket pitch they had a violent argument and swore they'd never speak to each other for the rest of their lives. One became the Rear Admiral, and one became the Archbishop, and they met on a station platform many, many years later. When the Archbishop saw the Admiral, he said to himself, "through the years I've taught my flock to love thy neighbour, I should speak to him, and I will." He strolled over and said, "I say, Station Master, what time does the next train leave?" Well, the Admiral was livid. He looked at his uniform, and he looked at the Archbishop and said, "In your condition Madam, you shouldn't even be travelling." Isn't that a classic story.

Another one they told me:

- There was a Texan, an Englishman, and a Frenchman in the lobby of a hotel in Paris. The Texan said, "you folks over here in France have a sayin' that we use in Texas. That sayin' goes like this: say, for instance, that I come home and find my wife in bed with another man, I'd say, 'excuse me.' That'd mean I have savoir-faire." The Englishman said, "I'm sorry old boy, but that's not quite correct. For instance, if I should come home and find my wife in bed with another chap, I should say, 'excuse me, continue.' Then I should have savoir-faire." The Frenchman said, "mes amis, zis is not correct, if I should come home and find my wife in bed wiz another man, I should tip my hat and say, 'excuse me, continue," and if he can continue, then he has savoire-faire."

The third one, actually I didn't hear this one from the man on the ship, I heard it from Commander Whitehead, he was the spokesman for Schweppes. Well, his story was kind of interesting:

Entertaining troops all over the world

- In the early 1900s in the Midwest of the United States there was a commotion when a young cowboy, either berserk or drunk came through the bat wing doors of a saloon, fired two shots into the floor and one into the ceiling and yelled out in a convincing voice, "I want every son-of-a-bitch out of here within 30 seconds." Well, you can imagine the furor, everybody grabbing for whatever aperture or chink they could find to get out of the room. When the dust settled, the cowboy leaned against the bar and rolled the gun on his finger and looked around and there was a little Englishman sitting in the middle of the room, sipping on a drink. The cowboy growled, "Well?" The Englishman said, "There were a lot of them, weren't there."

It's one thing to hear stories, but it's another thing to remember them and be able to tell them, but they come from great sources.

In one of our sojourns to entertain Canadian Forces we played every base in Canada where there were Canadian servicemen and women serving or training.

We were at the air training centre in Winnipeg and everybody who knows me says "Tell us a story" because they know I always have one that is appropriate. I'm not bragging, it just happens to be that way. There was a group, of maybe six or seven of us, watching some takeoffs and landings, or what they call touch-and-go in the training. They bring the plane in, touch it on the ground, and then take off again and do another circle, and so on and so on. And while we were talking I told them a story:

- this Air Canada captain had to have his semi-annual physical. And when the physical was finished, he was putting on his clothes, he said "How am I doc?" He said "You're in good shape Steve, but I'm going to ground you." He says "Ground me, what are you talking about?"

"Well, I don't know how to explain this to you, but you don't have depth perception. And this isn't something you have or don't have; it's something you don't have."

"Oh, come on," said the pilot, "look at all the millions of miles I've flown." "Yeah," said the doctor, "I know all about that." He said, "I want you to do something for me. I'm going to call a couple of guys in and we'll be a panel of three, and I want you to discuss something with me."

The pilot said "OK."

So the doctor called in two other fellows. "Now," he said, "Steve, what's

Gordie Tapp

Gordie rides a camel on the Sinai Peninsula.

happening is, that you're flying into, say, Toronto International Airport . . . you're at 31,000 feet, and you're ready to proceed with your landing. What do you do? What is your procedure?"

"Well," he said, "I start to take off power, and as I approach I notice that we have heavy overcast at 5,000 and I'm at 31,000 feet. So, as I'm taking off power I lock in on the localizer, and when I get below the cloud I take over visually. I call for flaps, half flaps, full flaps, wheels down, ease 'er in, ease 'er in, and when my first officer says 'Jesus Christ' I round out."

They all laughed. Rounding out is the same as rotating, which means the moment the nose of the airplane is pulled up, just before the wheels touch the runway. Rounding out is the phrase that they used back in those days, I guess.

One of the officers said to me 'Don't laugh Tapp, because you see that fellow right there, that's the way he flies.'

I looked at him and he had a patch over one eye; obviously only had one eye.

The officer then said, "As a matter of fact, if you look at the crown of that hangar there, that's what he rounds out on when he comes in."

I said, "What if he's not flying in here?" He said, "He only flies in here."

I'll never forget it because it was quite a laugh amongst the guys. I guess that was the way he was getting his mileage and keeping up his air hours, by flying into Winnipeg. We heard all kinds of stories like this as we were flying.

One night at nine o'clock, we took off from Edmonton, flying up to the Arctic. We were in a C-130, that's the Hercules, one of many, many, aircraft we flew in. It had canvas seats along the side, and we were all sitting on them laughing, talking, eating and drinking – not booze, maybe coffee or lemonade or something. Anyway, I say that because they were not booze sessions. Oh, I guess there were one or two guys who drank a little too much, but we didn't want to make a spectacle of ourselves.

In a track relative to that, we went into a bar one night with one of the fellows. He ordered a drink and then fell in front of the bar, and the bartender looked over the bar and said "Is he alright?" We said, "Yeah. Don't give him anymore to drink, he's our pilot." He really was one of the saxophone players, but that's how we used to have fun.

 Anyway, we took off from Edmonton, and after about two hours, we're laughing and talking and all of a sudden oil began to spray on us as we were sitting on the canvas seats along the side of the airplane.

There was a lot of commotion with the crew rushing back and forth, and, pleasantly, the captain came on and said 'Ladies and gentleman, we've got a problem; we've lost our hydraulics. Something is burst and our hydraulic oil is leaking. We're going to have to turn and go back."

So we turned around and started back. Now, without hydraulics, they had no power for steering, they had no power for flaps, they had no power for landing gear. Everything had to be done manually. They had to crank everything into position. It was a long evening, by the time we got back to Edmonton we had been in the air more than four hours.

Just to add to the excitement, when we landed we got a flat tire, a blow out. But we got safely to a halt and everybody got off and kissed the ground and

The original cast of Country Hoedown

thanked the Lord that we were safe.

We all loaded onto another C-130 and took off and finally made it up to Alert, which is the furthest point north where servicemen are stationed. It's about 250 miles south of the North Pole. At that time, it was at the height of the Cold War and that's where they listened to Russian transmission and we were closer to Moscow than we were to Toronto, and it kind of gives you an uneasy feeling, but those guys were so reliable, I swear by them. They were just marvellous.

It was not quite as easy as getting off one plane and right onto the other at Edmonton. The hydraulic fluid had been spilling onto us for a couple of hours. We all had to have showers and get our clothes washed before we could resume the trip.

I don't know how to explain this, probably a psychiatrist can, but I've always been a boob about being away from home.

I was homesick in the army. In fact, when I first went to Hollywood, I lived in Los Angeles, and I used to drive out Lacieniga Boulevard just to look at the Air Canada sign, and Archie Campbell used to say "Boy, you're something else."

Entertaining troops all over the world

And I asked him "You never feel homesick?" He said, "No, I never feel that way."

I said, "I stay in a motel room for two or three days and when I leave it I'm standing there looking at it like I'm leaving my home." I think it's a freak in my nature.

Relative to that, I must tell you a story. In our World Tour of 1967 we played a big show in New Delhi, and we were served all kinds of Indian dishes and so on. The night of the show, they had a big party, a big soiree, and we had all kinds of food. They told me this is good and this is good, and I tried it all. The next morning I was very sick. A couple of the others with our group were upset, too.

I went into the washroom and I was on my knees in there being very ill. I didn't pay attention to the time. When I finished, I came out and I started looking for our people and I couldn't find them anywhere. I went outside and our bus was gone, two buses actually.

I thought, "Holy smokes. They've gone and left me." So I tried to explain to the doorman that I needed a taxi. It took a while, but finally I got through to him.

The taxi driver said "Where do you want to go?" And I said "I want to go to the airport." He said "Which one?" And I thought, "Oh brother, I've had it."

I looked in my wallet, I had a few rupees, I had no American money, no credit cards. Just a few rupees. I didn't have enough for a cab fare. But I had to get to the airport.

We were held up by men with carts drawn by donkeys, and cattle on the road, and it took us a long time to get to the airport. As we pulled in the airport driveway I caught a glimpse of one of our aircraft with the maple leaf on the tail, and I want you to know I felt a great deal better.

I asked the driver to wait while I ran to find somebody. I came across one of the musicians, and I told him I needed some money and I went and paid the taxi driver.

Then I went looking for Mr. Dalziel, who was our liaison officer. "How come you left me?"

"I didn't know I left ya."

Gordie Tapp

"Well, don't you check the buses when people leave?"

"No, I thought you were there."

"Holy smokes, I could have been left."

Had this been a practical joke, I may have reacted differently, but this was genuine human error. You don't expect it to happen when you are on a group tour and it's hard to believe that it could happen on a show tour, where everyone knew each other.

I want you to know, I was a grown man, but I was pretty scared being left behind in a country where I didn't know the language and I didn't have any money and didn't have an itinerary.

Anyways, getting homesick is one of the quirks in my nature. I've never gotten over it, and I'm 84 years of age.

Gordie Tapp

The 1967 Centennial Year World Tour group, off to entertain Canadian servicemen, poses for this picture before take-off.

12

Caught in middle
of Six-Day War

We had great tours through the Middle East, I managed to be Master of Ceremonies from 1961 to 1964. I missed 1965, but was back again in 1966 and 1967.

In 1967, the Six Days War broke out. We were doing a show in Egypt in a place called El Ariche, which was at that time an Arab city. We did it for the base there, handled by the Yugoslav troops. That was their bivouac.

As we drove down I said to the guys, that I noticed the Egyptians had dug in their tanks, and made gun emplacements out of them. I guessed they planned to hit El Ariche anyway.

The thought was they wouldn't be hitting El Ariche because it was Arab. But right across the Red Sea was Israel. That was where they were going to fire. I noticed that all the Egyptian troops were in running shoes, and I told the guys, "Look, they're all wearing running shoes, I wonder if that means anything?" Well, in this case it did mean something, because the Israelis chased them all the way from El Ariche to the Suez Canal, and they did it in six days.

I'll never forget, they woke us at 5:30 in the morning, they said, "Get up, get your gear, we've got to get out of here, war has broken out."

Caught in the middle of Six-Day War

We got dressed and got on Volkswagen buses and headed for El Ariche. On the tarmac was our Canadian Air Force plane. We got all our equipment on and boarded at about 10:30 in the morning and we sat there until 4:30 in the afternoon.

Gordie shows 'great courage'

May 1967 I went to the Gaza with Gordie Tapp, Elwood Glover, hockey star Dick Duff, some entertainers and a magician to entertain the UN Troops. We were invited to stay with the Canadians and travel out to other UN contingents to put on shows. The second night we put on our first show and on the way the roads were a solid line of Egyptian soldiers, tanks and trucks passing our two buses and a jeep. The next morning we were told that everyone had to return to Canada, except cameraman Bob Cole and soundman Larry Morey.

We were all taken to El Ariche to get on a plane going to Cyprus and Cole and Morey were to go on to Beirut to meet CBC reporter Ron LaPlante and make our way to Israel.

Our UN Caribou aircraft taxied out to the runway and then was told to shut down engines as there was hostile aircraft nearby.

Watching the MIGs taking off by racing down the runway and lifting their wheels before climbing some entertainers stayed on board the UN plane. and were very nervous. Some stayed in the shade of the wing to keep cool.

Gordie Tapp kept telling jokes to keep people calm. Gordie truly showed great courage under this tense moment and I was very proud of him.

I returned to El Ariche with the Israeli Army during the Six-Day War and all the MIGs were smashed and the hangars wrecked by the Israeli Airforce.

Bob Cole,

Milton, former CBC cameraman

We all had towels wrapped around our necks because we were perspiring. It was about 115 degrees and they couldn't connect to any equipment to get the air conditioning working on the aircraft. The Egyptian MIG jets kept flying over, and when they flew over, they'd shift the plane, they'd fly over and go vrooom, and our airplane would vibrate.

Gordie Tapp

Our officer, who was a wing commander, stuck his head through the cabin door and said, "Buckle up, we're taking off." Somebody said, "I thought we didn't have permission." He said, "We don't have permission, but we can't sit here any longer. We'll have no fuel, we've got to go."

So we took off, and on each of our wing tips there was a MIG jet. We were waving at them, and they were waving at us. They flew us over to the border to Lebanon and then peeled off and left. We landed in Lebanon and arrangements were made for a Canadian plane to come and take us home. I think we came home in C-130s. They would not fly the whole Atlantic, so they took us first to a base in England where we could fuel up for the ride home.

Some of the tours were very exciting. The first ones in 1961/1962 were scary because our barracks had sandbags in the windows. We didn't see any actual fighting, but you just felt for the people the way they regarded the Israelis, they were worried about it.

Tommy Hunter and I were in our hut one day and two Arab boys were doing the cleaning, making the beds and so on. There was a map on the wall. I said, "Hey, Tom, look, there's a map, there's the Red Sea and there's Israel. I wonder if there are any guys from Canada in there?"

One of the Arab boys said, "You know Israeli?" We said, "No, but we know fellas who are fighting in the Israeli Army."

"And you like Israeli?"

We said no, "we're here to entertain the Swedes, the Norwegians and the British."

He was a little upset about it because he thought we had Jewish friends. Funny enough, one of our guys, our drummer, was Jewish, but his name was Mickey Shannon. He was accepted because his name was Shannon, but I guess he was Yiddish. We used to kid him. We'd say, "if you're not careful, we'll squeal on you."

We were driving around to the different outposts, and Mickey Shannon's hat blew off. He was riding in the back of the truck. He got the driver to stop, and he was running after his hat when all hell broke loose.

Soldiers were out with rifles, telling him to stop running and to not to move. He said, "What's the matter, I just want to get my hat?" They said, "Mines, all kinds of mines."

91

Caught in the middle of Six-Day War

Gordie, right, with Montreal Canadiens great Jean Beliveau on a beach during one of the trips to entertain Canadian troops.

We thought, "Holy Geez, poor Mick. Is he going to get out of there?" We all stood and watched while he slowly picked his way out without stepping on one.

When we went on these tours to the troops we would pick an orchestra, and Phil Nimmons would be the orchestra leader. A lot of very prominent Toronto musicians came with him. We'd take an eight or 10-piece. We had singers like Danielle Durice from Montreal, her sister Denise Anger, we took a magician with us by the name of Robert Downey, who later died in a head-on crash just outside Detroit. Downey was just an amazing magician and he was always doing tricks for us when we were waiting for something to happen. He did some wonderful tricks.

We took two French-Canadian performers who did a stump dance with broad axes that was kind of like a clog, a really great act. We all enjoyed it. One of them is still alive. In fact, I hear from him quite often, his name is Gilles Roy, and he was a great little guy. One day in Tanzania he saw us in a restaurant, he walked right through the window, but he never got a scratch.

He thought everything was open, Didn't realize there was any glass. He walked through the glass. Just didn't see it.

In 1967 the world tour was a magnificent experience. We played wherever there were Canadian servicemen or diplomatic corps, and it was just a magnificent experience. It was at that time that I was lucky enough to have tea with Indira Gandhi in New Delhi at the Canadian diplomatic home, with the High Commissioner and his wife.

A great experience.

Indira was aware that we were television people from Canada, and talked very diplomatically. She had a very quiet voice, you really had to listen. She also had an accent.

That trip lasted 31 days, we had two aircraft. There were 65 cast and crew, including people to take care of the wardrobe, and maintenance for our equipment. There were a lot of people. All the entertainers were in one plane and the technical crew flew in another.

We were coming back from Egypt and we stopped in Pisa, Italy, to refuel. There was quite a storm. I didn't think we'd be taking off, but the captain said that conditions were fine, and we did leave. We flew through that storm, and I'll never forget it, because with the flashes of lightning you'd look out and see the trees on the side of the mountain. I began to wonder if they were trying to knock the wings off. I went to sleep and I was awakened by one of the officers who said, "Mr. Tapp, would you please come forward, the captain would like to speak to you."

So I went forward to the cockpit. The captain said, "Gordie, you don't mind me calling you Gordie." I said, "No sir." He said, "We've run into a bit of a problem, Syria is at war with France, we're flying to Orly (Airport) in Paris, but we're not allowed to fly over continental France, they're not allowing any foreign aircraft to fly over continental France. So I'd like to know where you're

Caught in the middle of Six-Day War

Singing at a concert at RCAF headquarters in Downsview, Toronto, are Gordie, Pat Hervey, The Hames Sisters, John Davidson, the leader of the Singing Swinging 8, Tommy Hunter and Tommy Common.

going, and we'll land at the nearest base."

I said, "We're on our way to Hamer in Germany to do a show." He said, "I'll see if we can get a reasonable distance from Hamer." We got a long distance from Hamer, because we got to a place called Gutersloh, which was the headquarters for Goering and the Luftwaffe during the war.

To get to Germany we had to fly over the Alps, so we had to use oxygen masks. It was my job to go through the plane with a stick. Everyone had oxygen masks, but half the people were asleep and didn't realize the problem we were in. The first thing they'd do when they'd wake up was to reach for a cigarette, and I had to be there with a stick to stop them because you can't smoke when there's oxygen in the aircraft.

Anyway, when we landed, I was so pleased to land I got off and kissed the ground.

Gordie Tapp

They had the Vulcan hydrogen bomber stationed at Gutersloh. We were told when we were landing that no one was to go near it or to take photos of it. We go off, and our steel guitar player, Al Harris, who just passed away, took out a camera and took a picture. Immediately there were two guards on him, grabbed his camera, tore the film out, exposed it and threw it away. I said to Al after, "I don't know what's the matter with you. You heard what they said, 'don't take pictures,' and now look what you've done." He said, "yeah, but look at the good pictures I took." He didn't get them of the Vulcan bomber anyway.

I was called by a gentleman who said, "Can you do a show Friday night in Belleville?" I said, "well, it'll be very difficult because my wife and I are staying overnight at the hotel at Toronto airport because we're leaving early in the morning for Europe. The 150 kilometre drive back would be too much." He said, "Well, how would it be if we got you a limo?" I said, "Well that would be wonderful, because I could sleep." He said, "all right, the limo will be there at 3:30." So the limo was there, I got in, and the we took off. We got just to Pickering, about 20 kilometres away, when two guys in a sports car had gone under the back of a truck and were decapitated, just about 10 cars in front of us.

Well, you can imagine the delay on the road. It was in August, and it was a hot day. It was the afternoon and people were going to the cottage with their kids. The kids were all crying because they wanted water and were uncomfortable. There were no pop machines in the area. Cars were steaming and boiling over because they were running in the heat without moving.

They brought through an ambulance, two tow trucks and a fire engine and behind them was a police car. They were able to run up the side of the highway and have room to get in and take care of the problem. I said to the limo driver, "I'm going to stand outside, you might as well turn it off, you don't want it to overheat, we've got a long way to go."

He turned it off and we were standing outside as the police car went by. A policeman pointed out the window and said, "Gordie Tapp." They stopped, I said, "yes, sir." They said, "where are you going, Gordie?" I said, "I'm going to Belleville, I've got a show at 8 o'clock." They said, "you'll be here for five hours, so forget it." I said, "well, that's not too good, is it." He said, "do you think your man could turn this thing around?" I asked the chauffeur, he said, "if I get some help." We helped him.

The policeman said, "I have to go to the accident and make out a report. When I

Caught in the middle of Six-Day War

come back, I'll flash my lights, you guys pull in behind me and follow me." He took us out to the service road, up the service road and back onto the highway around the accident and we got there in time to do the show. Thank God for that policeman, a *Hee Haw* fan who was kind enough to let us through.

When I came back from the world tour in 1967 I had a swelling on the side of my tongue. It got quite large, about the size of my thumb. I went to the doctor. He examined me and said, "I want you to see a specialist." He sent me to see Dr. Love. He's still alive. He said, "Gordie, this has to come out, and it's got to come out right away. What are you doing Saturday?"

I said, "Saturday? You work on Saturday?"

He said, "I'll do this on Saturday."

I phoned the CBC because I was recording my radio show and I got the CBC to let me off on the Saturday. I told them the situation. Saturday morning, my wife took me to the hospital, They put me in a room, put the little hospital nightgown on. The nurse left me sitting there, and she left a little clipboard there so I picked it up, and it said, 'tumour on tongue.' I thought, "that's it, they'll cut off my tongue, I won't be able to tell jokes, I won't be able to work. That's how it is, nothing I can do about it."

They wheeled me in. Dr. Love came out, with the big lights, and I'm on the gurney. He said, "Now let's have a look at this thing," and he took a cloth and pulled my tongue out. He said, "Where's your doctor?"

With my tongue out I said "he's out in the hall." The doctor must have been able to understand what I said because he turned to the nurse and said, "get him in here."

So my doctor came in and he said to my doctor, "Look at this." My doctor took a look and immediately said to the guy with the pentathal, "Take that off his arm. Take him back to his room."

I was lying there, wondering "What's going on?" My doctor came in and said "He's not going to touch it Gordie. He wants you to come to see him in two weeks. He thinks it's going down."

It did go down, but I can remember sitting on the bridge over the stream on my farm, looking at the sun and the sky and the trees and thinking, 'tumour on tongue,' well that's the end of this. When I went back to see him, it had completely disappeared. He said, "it was an infection in your gland, your

Gordie Tapp

CANADA

PRIME MINISTER · PREMIER MINISTRE

Ottawa,
K1A   OA2,
March 15, 1974.

Dear Mr. Tapp:

      I have learned recently that among your services to Canadians as an entertainer 'par excellence', you have been involved in over thirty trips overseas to entertain Canadian Troops.

      May I offer you my warmest congratulations and sincere appreciation for this outstanding record. I hope that you will continue for many more years to share your talents with your characteristic spirit of generosity and goodwill.

Sincerely,

Mr. Gordon Tapp,
  c/o CBC,
    P.O. Box 500,
      Terminal A,
        Toronto, Ontario.

We're lucky to have this letter from the Prime Minister. Gordie threw it away by mistake and Helen recovered it from the garbage and ironed it flat again.

system has taken care of it. The interesting part of the whole thing is that I thought it was a tapeworm." I said, "a tapeworm in my mouth?" He said, "it's not at all uncommon for them to start in the tongue area, and when they're ready for food they'll go to the intestine."

Caught in the middle of Six-Day War

I was thankful I didn't have to have an operation.

This reminded me of the East Indian gentleman who was in hospital with tubes and hoses out of every aperture in his body. He wore an oxygen mask over his mouth. The nurse came in to take care of the wires and meters, tucked him in and turned to leave. He said through the oxygen mask 'may you please tell me if my testicles are black or white?'

The nurse said, 'I beg your pardon?'

He repeated, still wearing the oxygen mask, 'may you please tell me if my testicles are black or white?'

She rolled the covers back and fondled him.

The gentleman pulled off his mark and said, 'thank you very much, I really enjoyed it, but you may have misunderstood me. Can you tell me please if my test results came back alright?'

I couldn't resist popping that one in there. It loses a bit in the translation, there's no way to muffle the voice in print, but I thought you'd get the picture and enjoy it just the same.

Another time when I left Cyprus to come home the boys gave me a carboy of wine. It was a big carboy - probably 24 or 25 bottles of wine - and it was all covered with wicker. It was a beautiful thing. I said, "I'll never get this through customs." They said, "try, make a fool of yourself." So I made out a card, and it said on it: 'To Gordie from the 53rd Wreckies. Thanks for all your entertainment, we look forward to seeing you when we get back to Canada.'

I brought it through and the customs guy said, "you can't bring that wine in here." I said, "I know, and I'm sorry about that, but the guys gave it to me, there's a tag on there." They read the tag and said, "ahh shit, that's ok, take it and drink it, just don't drink it all at once." So I brought it home, and it lasted a long time, it was great wine. It was called Othello. It's from Cyprus, good wine.

Donnie Johnson was one of the fine Canadian trumpet players, we worked together a lot. He used to do my old television show *PM Party* and then he was often on *What's On Tapp?* on network radio.

On one tour we were in Cyprus and Donnie bet the guys he could play *Taps* on any piece of pipe they brought to him. It was a pretty big bet, too.

One of the guys, an armourer in the outfit, brought him a Lee-Enfield rifle

Gordie Tapp

barrel. By gosh, he played *Taps* on it and won the bet.

Another time, I said to him, 'can you play *Trumpeter's Holiday*?' And he said, 'yeah,'

'I must get you to play it for me sometime.' He said, 'what room are you in?' I said, '208.'

I never thought any more of it. When I got to my room Ken Dalziel was packing things up. Ken was the organizer of all the shows that went overseas, and travelled everywhere with us. He was one of the officials at the CBC that arranged these things with the Department of National Defence. Anyways, he said, "we've been moved upstairs. This room was too small for the two of us, so they've moved us upstairs."

Finally, we went up to our new room. Soon I hear, tut-ta-la-tut-da-da-da-da tut-ta-la-tut-da-da-da-da daaa, and I thought, 'holy smoke, Donnie's playing that song for me, I bet he's at the old room.' So I ran down the hall, down the stairs, and looked down the hall, and there's Donnie standing in front of the door playing the song. The door flies open and there's a big Turk with a big handlebar mustache. He must have been about six-four standing there, glaring at Donnie.

Donnie just kinda tut- ta - la - tuted and then turned and walked down the hall. I don't think he ever forgave me. He didn't believe me that I had not set him up. I thought it was funny, so did others - all except Donnie and the big Turk. But I had no way of knowing, it was a funny experience.

We had some funny things happen when we were staying at the Elandulus Hotel in Gaza during our first tour in 1961.

There was a special safety chest/wardrobe in each room and the key was as big as your hand.

We were going to a function and Tommy Hunter dropped a cufflink. It went under the chest.

When we moved the chest we noticed that the chest did not have a back to it. It was placed flush with the wall. So the key was unnecessary and it wasn't a place where we left valuables after that.

The toilets were a little different than ours. There was a hole in the floor and two leather handles to hold on to as you squatted.

If anything splashed on the floor it got on your feet, so they had two blocks of wood with big pieces of rubber tire over them in a loop. It looked a little like a mule bedroom slipper. Leaving your shoes on, you slipped your feet into these blocks and usually they kept your feet dry.

When I saw these I thought it was so amusing I got a broom and picked them up and took them down the hall to a room where the Rhythm Pals were staying.

I opened the door and threw them inside and yelled 'You guys left your slippers in the washroom.'

I got their i m m e d i a t e attention as they were trying to kick them out of the room. Luckily, they didn't kill me.

Gordie as Gaylord, the MC for *Main Street Jamboree*.

Library and Archives Canada / Gordie Tapp Collection

The Rhythm Pals (Jack Jenson, Mark Wald and Mike Firby) were great guys and we had a lot of fun together on our many tours.

13

Sharing a car with a tiger!

I have had many opportunities to promote various things from cigarettes to cars in all kinds of media - radio, television and newspaper advertisements. I just don't remember the year, but I was doing a commercial for Brylcream and we used an English sports car in the commercial – it was an MG convertible. In fact, I took it in lieu of money for that commercial.

I drove it for some time until a guy tried to get in it with his car and then I traded it on a Chrysler Imperial. It was an interesting commercial because we used a tiger to demonstrate the smoothness of Brylcream, if you can imagine.

They wanted the tiger to sit in the MG, so they put a piece of meat in there. It was about eight pounds of beef, no fancy wrapping, not frozen, right on the front seat. The idea was to tempt the tiger to get into the car.

The tiger had other ideas. He never got in the car, but he tore the front seat out, and the bolts were as big around as my forefinger. It just pulled the whole thing right out. I watched in amazement and I said to the guys, "I don't care what you do, I'm not doing this commercial with that tiger."

He was a real tiger from the Toronto Zoo, and his name was Danny.

A guy came in, a staging guy, and said "We have some thick Plexiglas, Let's put the Plexiglas between Tapp and the tiger." And we shot the commercial.

Sharing a car with a tiger!

They had a lot of difficulty because the lighting was reflecting off the Plexiglas, But they got it fixed so there was no extreme light and we got the commercial done.

There I was standing beside the car with the tiger right there, just like he was at my elbow. There's quite a good ending to this story, let me take a minute and tell you.

We had Jacques Gauthier, an announcer from Montreal, to do the French version of the commercial. Our director said to me "Gordie, Jacques has to catch the plane at noon to go back to Montreal, do you mind if he does the commercial first?" And I said "No, of course not" And the commercial opened with us saying . . . "Hello, I'm Gordie Tapp . . . " Jacques had to do it in French of course.

He finished the commercial, we all shook hands and he left to get the airplane. And the director said "Now before we break for lunch, we've got time for one shot. I want you to get up there, Gordie, and do it exactly the way Jacques did it. You get it?" And I said "Yeah, no problem."

So I got up and then he yelled "Action," and I said "Bonjour, ici Jacques Gauthier" and the director said 'What are you doing?' I said 'You told me to do it exactly the same as Jacques...' He said "Get out of here! Let's break for lunch."

I did the last television commercial for Mark Ten cigarettes. In fact, it was the last cigarette smoking television ad, before they put the ban on smoking and they cut all smoking advertising from television.

We went out to shoot it in Vancouver. It was raining when we arrived on Tuesday. It rained on Wednesday, Thursday, Friday, Saturday, and finally the crew said, "If we're going to shoot this, we're going to have to shoot this thing in the airport." We did, going up and down on the escalator at the airport. The guys in the crew said, "We're sorry, but this (the rain) is not common."

I said, "hold on, I think this is very common." They said, "What do you mean?" I said, "Even your flag, your British Columbia flag only has half a sun on it." And they laughed.

I was spokesman for the state of Moralos in Mexico, and a spokesman for the Canadian Retirement Lifestyle Association and ETFS – Extra Travel Financial Services or Security and Canadian Snowbirds Association.

I started with CSA and had four years with them before getting an offer I couldn't refuse from the others. Now I'm back with CSA travelling all over the United States where Canadian seniors migrate in winter, leaving the snow shovelling for their offspring and the mitts and toques back home. Naturally, I get to play the hot spots in California, Arizona, Texas and Florida. It's a great experience and I enjoy it. What other employers pay you to go on 'vacation?'

Don't get me wrong, I don't regard my work with CSA as a holiday as such. But I am one of those few people who have a job that they absolutely love. I know what it's like working for a living when you don't particularly like what you are doing - I did my time in the shoe factory in London. It just wasn't for me and I am so glad that my wife encouraged me to go back to Lorne Greene for a second interview and that he told me my entertainment career wasn't going anywhere - at least with him - unless I went back to school to finish my high school education.

While doing the snowbird extravaganza in Florida I met a man named Dennis Rankin who was publicist for Mexico's tourism. And, of course, he was on the show to invite people – seniors – to go to Mexico and buy condos.

He asked me one day if I would be interested in promoting a project that he was doing. And I said "Well, what is it?" He said "Well, I'll take you to Mexico and show it to you." So he did and we went to a place called Cuernauaca, it's called the city of eternal spring and it's most beautiful. They were building a complex there, and I won't mention any names but we picked out the one that

Sharing a car with a tiger!

we wanted, Helen and I, and that was to be the arrangement for payment.

We looked the whole situation over and it was really beautiful. In fact, if we looked off our front porch, we were looking at Popocatepetl, which was 80 miles away, a volcano that still is active, and you could see the steam rising out of it. I was really fascinated with it. We weren't in the hills, but we could see the hills and the mountains out to the south and west of us. Sixty miles away was Acapulco. It was a very beautiful spot. I was very enthralled with it.

I got busy learning my Spanish and was doing quite well, but Helen just wasn't convinced that she wanted to be away in a place that's foreign. Anyway we walked away from it and returned to Canada.

Denis came to me a year or so ago and said he wanted me to do a tourism film for Durango. We spent about a week shooting. Durango is a magnificent state. They have a canyon there that's bigger than the Grand Canyon. You could put the Grand Canyon in it a couple of times, I think. Beautiful waterfalls, great fishing, particularly big bass, and some of the greatest scenery you'd ever want to look at.

But they have never had tourism in Durango. My trip was done through the governor. We had several meetings with the governor. He was quite an interesting man. And they're using it now as the tourism ploy to attract visitors. Tourism is a good money maker for Mexicans. And I'm sure that Durango will catch on just like all the other favourite hot spots.

Right now I'm waiting to hear from Dennis because he has another plan in mind.

Gordie was a spokesman for International Harvester, promoting farm implements, trucks and tractors and was on the cover of their magazine in 1975.

Gordie Tapp

This picture was one of the advertisements when I was spokesman for Yamaha in Canada. I travelled all across Canada, from Halifax to Vancouver. Wherever they had stores I was there doing the promotion thing, signing autographs. They were always talking about taking me to Japan, but they never did.

When the president of Yamaha came over from Japan, his name was Ioka, I said to one of the guys, I'd like to have my picture taken with the president. He asked why. I said, "Well, it would be nice to have, and it would be a picture of Tapp-Ioka (Tapioca). He said, "My gosh." We told Mr. Ioka that, he didn't know anything about tapioca, so it didn't mean anything to him. I never did get my picture taken with him.

Friends you meet riding a Harley

Gordie and his Harley were used as the poster and billboard for the president's ride when the Harley-Davidson president in Toronto led a trip into the Muskokas for lunch for Harley owners in Ontario.

14

Friends you meet riding a Harley

When I was a boy, 10 or 12 years-old, our next door neighbour, Joe Coombs, had a Harley-Davidson motorcycle. Joe would take me for a ride on it occasionally, and I was much enamoured with that machine. When he wasn't around I would just sit and look at it.

He had a friend who came over and he also had a Harley, and the two of them used to ride together.

It's hard to believe, but, many years later, I'd be in my late 20s working at CHML in Hamilton selling my own time on *What's on Tapp?* my radio show at 10:30 at night, I met this Harley rider.

I was in the Harley-Davidson dealership out on Parkdale in Hamilton and this man came over and asked me if he could help me. I told him I was just looking, but asked him if he was interested in advertising, I told him about my show and asked him to listen to it. He looked very familiar, and I said "Do I know you?" And he said "I don't know," and I said "Where are you from?" He said "London." And I said "Did you have a friend named Joe Coombs, who used to ride Harley with you?" "Yeah," he said "I still see Joe occasionally. He's living up around Sauble Beach some place."

Friends you meet riding a Harley

Ron Patterson, left, with Gordie and their prized Harleys.

Well, I was really amazed. I said "Would you remember the 12 year-old kid that used to hang around and look at the bikes when you guys would come in?" He said, "Yes. He lived next door?" I said "That's right and that was me. What was your name?" He said, "Pool, Percy Pool." And I was in Pool's Harley-Davidson on Parkdale. Today it is owned and operated by Bill Leslie, a good friend.

Anyway, Percy bought some radio time from me, and I was telling him my interest in motorcycles. I got my standing orders in the army when I was about 22 I guess, riding a BSA, a motorcycle made in England by British Small Arms, used for messenger service, and reconnaissance. Dispatchers also rode them.

Anyway, when I became interested in motorcycles I got into a business with two young fellows called Perth Sports, up in Stratford. And I bought a Yamaha 650, and I rode it for a while, then I had a 750 Honda for a time.

Then I went to Percy Pool and I bought my first Harley and I rode them for about 40 years. I had five of them over the course of time. But when I turned 80 I figured I'd better be careful because they take a lot of attention and the traffic is different than it used to be. So I sold it.

But I tell you I miss it, and when I hear one go by me now with that throaty

Gordie gets ready to do a television commercial for Ultramatic in Ron's personal, mirrored bedroom.

sound, it sure brings back a lot of memories.

I was on a poker ride one time. That's a ride that about 100 motorcyclists get involved in, and they usually do it for some cause. One I did many times was Ride For Sight - a ride to raise funds for the blind. Once I was parade marshal, and won a telephone that I am still using, because I was the oldest rider - at that time I was 73.

I met a fellow, on a ride and we began talking - and started a relationship that has gone on for more than 20 years.

His name was Ron Patterson. "What do you do?" He said "I have a bed company. I call my business Ultramatic Sleep." And he said "You wouldn't be

Friends you meet riding a Harley

Gordie and Helen loved to don their leathers and ride their Harley.

interested in being a spokesman for us, would you?" And I said "Gee, yeah, I would. I'd like to look into the situation, because I don't like to do something sight unseen, I'd like to know about it."

So he invited me to visit him at his office and warehouse in Burlington. By golly, little did I know that 22 years later I'd still be doing Ultramatic commercials, and I'm proud to be doing them because it is a really wonderful product.

The interesting part of this whole thing is that Ron and I had struck up a friendship that has lasted all these years. He still rides, he's got three Harleys. In fact, he had one built that is just magnificent. It's got pants over the wheels and oh gosh it's a gorgeous looking thing, all in gold.

When we started doing commercials we used Ronnie's bedroom quite a bit. And the reason for this is that they had Ultramatic beds in their bedroom, and it was a beautiful bedroom. It was on quite a nice estate in the north end of

Burlington that he had built himself.

He had the whole ceiling done in mirror. And he said to me "What do you think of it?" And I said "Well, it's great I guess." But I said " I get a kick out of the little sign down in the corner." And he said "What sign's that?" I said "The one down in the corner that says 'objects viewed in this mirror are not as large as they appear.'"

He got a great kick out of it, and that's been a constant joke with us for a number of years.

Gordie rode his Harley until he was 80. Helen quit riding the pillion when she was 75.

Ron Patterson, owner and general manager of Ultramatic. A great guy, and a manufacturer of a very, very, fine product.

I am not just saying that. I have five Ultramatic beds; four that I have purchased – and that's the truth –and one that Ron gave me when Helen had two of her hips replaced. It helped her get in and out of bed when she was recuperating and it certainly helped her a lot so we keep that one down in Burlington in our apartment along with the two in our bedroom, and then we have two up here at the farm.

Ron still runs the business along with his wife Donna. She's an essential part of the business and a nice lady. It's great to be associated with them.
You can't meet Ron and not like him.

These three Gordie characters were part of a CBC promotion.

Library and Archives Canada / Gordie Tapp Collection

15

'Sing 'em a good song, Gordie' says Canadian Prime Minister

You know in this business you get the opportunity to meet a lot of wonderful people. I was coming out of Saskatoon and it was before Air Canada had the loading ramps. You had to walk out onto the tarmac and up the stairs into the aircraft. I was walking with my guitar, and someone behind me said, "Sing 'em a good song, Gord." I turned around and it was Prime Minister John Diefenbaker.

I was kind of impressed that he should speak to me in that kind of a friendly manner, so comfortable, just like we were old buddies. I met him again later on when his beloved Conservatives were the Opposition and he was a back-bencher, although still affectionately called 'Dief The Chief.' I was out in Prince Albert, Saskatchewan, his old stomping grounds, to do a thing for the Saskatchewan Fish and Game Association. I was in the studio in the morning at 8 o'clock recording some promotion for it when Dief came out of the studio, he'd been in there being interviewed.

He came out of the studio and said, "Ahh yes, Tapp." He came over and we chatted. I said, "How are you getting along with our leader?" He did the most wonderful impression of Pierre Trudeau, who was Prime Minister of Canada at the time. and he pranced around the lobby, and I tell you we were on the floor laughing.

It's great to meet these people, it really is. When we went to India in 1967, it was Canada's birthday and we went around the world doing shows for Canadian servicemen and diplomatic corps.

I would say I did about 200 shows from 1959 to 1972, all over the world for Canadians, wherever they were stationed. 1959 was a trip to Resolute Bay and the Arctic. Our first overseas tour was in 1961.

When we were in India in 1967 and I met Indira Gandhi, what a delightful person.

We were at Canada House in India with High Commissioner Rolly Michener, who went on to become the Governor General of Canada.

Same trip, different country, we had a marvellous trip to the Aswan Dam. Egypt's world famous High Dam was an engineering miracle when it was built in the 1960s. It contains 18 times the material used in the Great Pyramid of Cheops. The Dam is more than two miles long, half-a-mile thick at the base and stands 364 feet tall. It provides irrigation and electricity for the whole of Egypt, together with the old Aswan Dam built by the British between 1898 and 1902 just a few miles down river.

Standing on the The High Dam there are spectacular views of Lake Nasser, which is 500 miles long and at the time it was built was the world's largest artificial lake.

Our guide was with General Chicaoui (pronounced Chickowee) of the Egyptian army. I heard that during the Six-Day War that he had been captured and released, but Colonel Elie who took me all through Cairo, lost his life during that campaign.

Perhaps the highlight of my career was performing for the Duke of Edinburgh. I told a story, originally told to me by Bernard Braden, a Canadian who was a well-known British broadcaster.

During King George and Queen Mary's visit to Canada in 1939 a man gave King George a note. The King put the note in his pocket and didn't read it until he was getting ready for bed.

The note writer wanted to know why the Royal train was not stopping near Blind River on the North Shore of Lake Superior.

Gordie Tapp

The King asked the question why the train was passing through and was told that no stop was scheduled because it would be the middle of the night.

The King decided that the train should stop because there would be people at the station watching the train go through.

As the train approached the community, the King and Queen both awakened from their sleep. They got dressed and walked out onto the special platform on the train as it pulled into the station.

There was no-one around. Then a man appeared and the King asked him if he was the one who had written the note.

He said he was. The King asked him what he did and he said he was the reeve of the municipality.

"What's a reeve?" asked the King.

"It's like a mayor," said the reeve.

"Do you wear a chain of office?" asked the King.

"I do," said the reeve, "but only on special occasions."

After our show the Duke said he wanted to talk to me about one of my stories.

Well, I knew which one.

He was so polite. He said he liked the show and he was aware of the story, but said that when the Queen told the story she said it occurred somewhere in Quebec.

Who's going to argue with the King and Queen. What a great story wherever it occurred.

Gordie Tapp

Gordie with Ray Price. Gordie still sings Ray's song, *You're The Best thing That Ever Happened To Me,* when he performs - especially when his wife, Helen, is in the audience.

Ferlin Husky introduced Gordie to hunting, but he couldn't get interested in it. Gordie and Ferlin remained great friends.

Gordie Tapp

Roy Clark and Gordie on the set of *Hee Haw* . . . and Roy's special words for Gordie

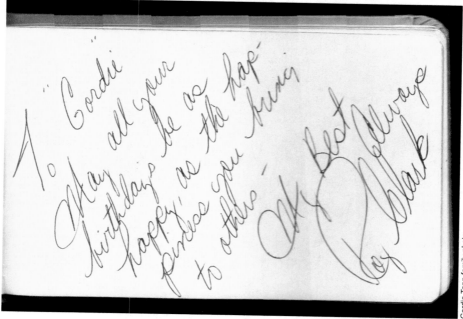

Gordie Tapp

Buck Owens liked to work with Gordie, on the right in overalls, with the entire *Hee Haw* cast..

Library and Archives Canada / Gordie Tapp Collection

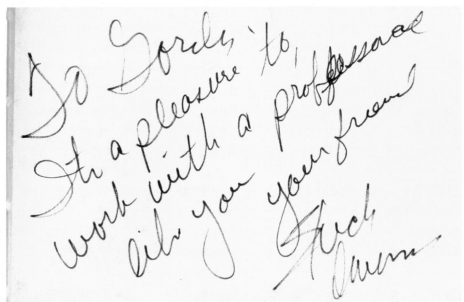

Gordie Tapp family photo

16

Working with some great people

I have worked with some terrific entertainers - and many real characters. *Hee Haw* opened the door to so many opportunities for me, sometimes I wonder whether all this really happened to me. There have been some phenomenal people. In this chapter I'll tell you some of the stories.

We had an act - I won't mention his name, we'll call him Johnny. Johnny was unusual. He played fiddle and he did bird sounds, and he did a lot of tricks with the fiddle. He was a guest several times on the *Dean Martin Show*. But he was really quite a character and I hit it off with him very well. We chummed around and we'd have a drink together.

I said to him one day - I think we were playing the Pennsylvania State Fair – "Do you know any of the girls in the chorus line?" "Oh yeah," he said "and I've had half of them." I said, "You what?" He said, "I've had half of them." I said "Johnny!" He reasoned, "Well, what the hell."

We wandered over to the grandstand where the girls were working out and they were staging. I said "And you've had half of them. My, you're some man." "Yeah, you see the one second from the end on the right hand side?" And I said "Yeah." He said, "I'm having her now."

That's the kind of character he was. He flew his own plane and was quite a

Working with some great people

Hee Haw cast on set

pilot, I guess. He had a little computer aboard that told him - among other things - how much gas he had and how many miles he had to fly. And not long after that engagement, he and his wife were flying to another engagement and I guess he miscalculated because he didn't have enough gas, and they went down with the plane. Both he and his wife were lost in the crash. But he certainly was a character to know. There were a lot of them, a lot of them.

At the Rocky Mountain Jamboree with Tammy Wynette

I recorded a song for Tammy Wynette's third or fourth husband, I'm not sure which. He was the Director of Music on the *Hee Haw* show. I was at their house one morning, My wife, Helen, was with me. We were sitting having

120

coffee, and were going over the contract for me for my recording. Tammy came down the stairs in a chenille housecoat with her hair all up in curlers. I was so used to seeing Tammy at her best for performances. I guess it was normal, but sometimes it is hard to accept. It just looked odd seeing one of country music's favourite people, famous for her beautiful hair as well as her music, standing there with her hair in curlers.

Tammy and I were entertaining at the Rocky Mountain Jamboree and Tammy just finished doing her eight songs or so and taking applause. I held her hand and we walked back and took bows, and then I let go of her hand and picked up the microphone and said "Ladies and gentleman, may I present Charlie Daniels . . ." and 500 motorcycles started up.

You never heard such a roar in your life. Tammy said "What are we going to do?" I said "We're going to get the hell out of here because if they come on stage there's going to be no room for us."

We ran back to the stage door. It was a funny situation, but those kind

George Jones joins Cousin Clem on *Hee Haw*.

of things happened. I remembered prior to starting the show they had nude women dancing out in front of the stage. A policeman came over and chased them away and stopped all that nonsense. I guess the girls were half loaded with coke or something.

Playing Wembley Stadium with George Jones

After Tammy Wynette and George Jones D-I-V-O-R-C-E became final, George married a girl named Nancy. George and I played the big country music show

Working with some great people

in the old Wembley Stadium in London, England. It was one of my toughest gigs trying to do country jokes to those English people, so I quickly got to English stories and made it work. No corn pone jokes for them. The British have such a wonderful sense of humour. It's so different from ours in North America. Give them something clever, subtle, perhaps tied to a current event, and they are happy.

Henny Youngman invites Gordie to New York for lunch!

Henny Youngman was a master of the one-liner. His classic, of course, was "Take my wife - please!'

For years it was suggested we get him on *Hee Haw,* but it was felt that he didn't fit our format because he didn't do rural humour. I suggested that if we put him in overalls we could probably make it work. We did make it work, and we became pretty good friends.

One day I was working in the barn. The phone rang and Helen picked it up in the house, I was on the extension in the barn. A voice said "Gordie?" I said "Yeah."

"This is Henny."

"Yeah Henny, how are you doing?"

"What are you doing?"

I said "I'm shovelling horse manure."

He said "You're always shovelling shit."

"Nah, you mean with my mouth. Anyway, what can I do for you?"

"I want you to be my guest at noon hour today at the Park Plaza in New York."

"Well, Henny, I don't know whether I've got time, it's after 7:30."

He said "Get your ass to the airport." So I hung up and said "Helen, put some stuff in a bag and get dressed, we're going to New York to visit Henny." So we flew to New York. Henny met us at the airport, took us home to his apartment with Sadie, and said to Helen "Now you stay here with Sadie, Gordie and I are going to the Park Plaza."

It was the 35th anniversary of Milton Berle on television and there were more personalities in the audience than I had seen in one place before. I had so much fun. Henny and I sat at a table with Henny's manager with Bill Cosby, Peter Falk and a Chrysler dealer from the New York area.

Eddy Arnold always wanted an English story

Eddy Arnold was responsible for getting me on the Mike Douglas show. He asked Mike to bring me on, convincing Mike that he would like my English stories.

Whenever I was near Eddy he always said, "Give me an English story." He liked English stories.

I was on the Mike Douglas show three times. The last

Gordie with Eddie Arnold and Lee Clayton, one of secretaries with *Hee Haw*.

time I was a guest, Sam Levenson was also on. He's passed away now, rest his soul, and as you know, just last year Mike Douglas died.

Sam was a wonderful comic, he was a school teacher and in his act he used a lot of the things that happened in school. He tied a lot of the stories into his own life, giving it a very humourous background. For instance, they were studying anatomy, and he brought the skeleton home that they were using in the classroom and he hung it on the hook behind the door in his bedroom. One morning, his mother said to him, "Shmuel," (that's what she called

Working with some great people

him) "you've got someone in your room." He said, "No mother, that's just a skeleton, we're studying it." She said, "Bring him down, I'll give him some chicken soup." His stories were wonderful.

Perrola remembers Gordola after 16 years

Sam called me Gordola. Now Gordola is a friendly expression in Jewish. For instance, John, would be Johnola, Michael, Michaelola, David, Davidola. You get the picture? Perry Como was on the show, and he called him Perrola. Well, 16 years later, and this is the truth, I was emceeing the Shrine Golf Tournament for Foster Brooks in Louisville, Kentucky, and our special guest was Perry Como. I said, "Ladies and gentlemen, the world's most renowned Italian barber, Perry Como!"

Perry came up on stage and said, "Gordola." I said, "Perrola, you remembered!" He did, he was a wonderful man, very warm and very gentle, and very pleasant to be with.

Library and Archives Canada / Gordie Tapp Collection

Plenty of stars out for Billy Barty's bar scene

There are a lot of stars in this picture: Curly Putnam, the guy who wrote 'oh, the old town looks the same as I stepped down from the train *(The Green, Green Grass of Home)*' is standing right behind Grandpa Jones. Sam Lovullo, *Hee Haw* producer is second from the left, standing in front of Gordie. Ernie Borgnine, Fred McMurray and his wife June Haver, Jim Bacon, the columnist are all in the picture. Billy Barty is in the front beside George Lindsay.

124

Gordie Tapp

Let me tell you a story about Billy Barty that happened at this event. We were finished playing the golf game and we went into the bar, it was kind of an outdoor bar. We were sitting on stools, and there was Ken Curtis, Festus from *Gunsmoke,* and Ernie Borgnine having a beer.

Billy came in and climbed up onto the stool, got his stomach on the stool and his feet and legs were wobbling like he was trying to

Gordie with country music sweetheart Barbara Mandrell.

swim. We grabbed a hold of him and sat him up on the seat properly. He ordered another beer. The bartender went to the other end of the bar, Billy didn't get his beer.

About 10 minutes later, Billy jumped up on the bar and ran down the bar, knocking people's beer over. But that didn't bother him.

He grabbed the bartender by the scruff of the neck and he pulled him up over the edge of the bar and said, "I wanna know where my beer is,

Country singer Denise Tapp (no relation) met Gordie at an event in North Carolina.

Working with some great people

Ronnie Milsap, when he did this *Pfft You Was Gone* skit on *Hee Haw*, told Gordie, "Don't stand on my blind side." Gordie says even though he is blind, Ronnie was able to move around the stage by counting the steps he was taking. "He used to scare us by going right to the edge of the stage," says Gordie, "then stopping and saying, 'oh, that's about as far as I should go.' Gordie said Ronnie was marvellous and "he used to like having fun with us."

I ordered a beer 10 minutes ago and you haven't sent it to me," and then he pushed him back down into place.

The guy looked pretty shook up, but the place was in fits of laughter. Billy ran down and got back on his stool again.

Senator a Hee Haw fan

I was flying out of Chicago a number of years ago, on my way to Nashville. They seated me in seat 3A, I'd just got comfortably ensconced in my seat when the flight attendant (they were stewardess' back then) came over and said, "Mr. Tapp, could you move into number 3B?" I said, "It doesn't matter to me, not at all. What's the problem?" She said, "It's not a problem, but we have a member of the legislature who always rides in that seat and they just inadvertently gave it to you."

A short time later a man got on, wearing a grey suit, with silver hair and horn-

Library and Archives Canada / Gordie Tapp Collection

Gordie at the Grand Ole Opry with Roy Acuff to greet a number of Canadian visitors to the Nashville show.

rimmed glasses. He had a *Washington Post* under his arm. He sat down in 3A, opened his newspaper and started to read. I was reading a book at the time, so I just continued.

When the stewardess came to serve us lunch, she folded out the tables and put the napkins on them. He reached over and touched me on the knee and said, "Are you on that funny show?"

I said, "Yes sir, I guess I am."

He said, "Well, we see you in our house, and we sure do enjoy it."

I said, "Thank you sir, but you have the advantage of me."

He said, "I'm sorry, I'm Senator (J. William) Fulbright (of Arkansas)."

I said, "Oh, Chairman of the Ways and Means committee."

He said, "You know more about me than I do."

I've said, to my wife several times, "You fly, you look down and you see several antennas, and you think, those people are probably watching me on Saturday night. You never know who's watching you. Television is such a marvellous medium."

Working with some great people

Gordie Tapp family photo

Alabama Governor George Wallace, a big fan of *Hee Haw*, shakes Gordie's hand at a golf tournament in Montgomery.

Governor Wallace a big Hee Haw fan

I've probably played in 30 or 40 pro-celebrity golf tournaments over my period on *Hee Haw*. Goober used to have a tournament in Montgomery, Alabama, and I played it for many years. Each year governor George Wallace used to have a breakfast for all the people that performed or played in the tournament.

As you approached the big line up of people going in, the governor himself was sitting in his wheelchair. This, of course, was after his accident. He had a Major Domo standing beside him, a big black man, good-looking man, in a uniform. He had a staff in his hand, and as you approached he hit the staff three times on the floor ... Bang! Bang! Bang! ... and he'd turn to the governor and say ' Governor, this is ... ' and he would name the person coming up to meet Governor Wallace. Well, he hit the staff three times for me and said "Mr. Governor, this is ..." and George Wallace reached up and took my hand and, turning to Major Domo, said "You don't have to tell me who this man is, I see him every week on

Gordie met Governor Wallace's third wife, Lisa Taylor, a country music singer - and a big fan of Hee Haw - at the golf tournament in Alabama. The governor at Lisa married in 1981 and divorced in 1987.

television." I felt kind of good about that.

I said, "You know, Mr. Governor, we heard that after your accident, when you gained consciousness, the first thing you asked for was a television so you could watch *Hee Haw*.' And he said, "And that's a fact."

Gordie met many sports stars

Cousin Clem serenades former Toronto Maple Leafs captain Darryl Sittler on a television show.

Gordie met New York Yankees pitcher Virgil Trucks at a celebrity golf tournament. They became good friends. I told him about going to see him play in Detroit with my dad. Mom had packed a pair of binoculars and wrapped them in the colour comics from a newspaper. A piece of paper got stuck onto the lens and I thought Little Orphan Annie was pitching for Virgil for the first three innings. Virgil liked that story when I told him several years later.

Gordie talks with former Toronto Maple Leafs captain George Armstrong on a stage overseas entertaining Canadian servicemen.

Gordie Tapp

The day I out-drove Roger Marris

I once out-drove baseball's big slugger Roger Marris, in a golf tournament in Tulsa, Oklahoma.

It was very, very, dry. It was so dry that I told everybody that I saw the trees running around looking for a dog, they needed water so badly.

But it was one of those days when the golf ball bounces and rolls, seemingly for ever on a bone hard course. This day I was particularly lucky because the long drive hole was on a down slope. My kind of hole, for sure.

My drive went up the side of a hill then started to roll down. And as it rolled down, it rolled forward, down and forward. And it kept going, kept going, kept going, and it ended up about two inches past the long drive marker.

I looked at the marker and it said 'Roger Marris.' So there was a marshal out there, and he asked me my name, and we talked about *Hee Haw*, and he put my name on the flag.

When I came in, Marris came over and said, 'Hey, Tapp, was that your name on the long drive flag?' I said "Yeah." "Hell," he said "You couldn't out-dive me in a cart."

I said "You're right, Roger, but I went up on that hill and it was dry and it just kept rolling, and there it was two inches in front of your ball."

We had a good laugh over it. We got to be good friends, and had dinner together – along with Mickey Mantle – and had a lot of laughs.

Our meal was a long time coming, and Mickey said "Gee, I didn't know it was going to take this long." I said, "It better hurry up or I'm going to have to go back to the hotel and shave. "And he really laughed. He said, "Imagine thinking of that."

At Goobers golf tournament in Birmingham, Alabama, we arrived at the 10th tee and there was a waiting period., Drinks and hors d'oeuvres were being served by the Dallas Cowgirls. I saw coach Bear Bryant, of the Alabama Crimson Tide, who only had one losing season in 38 seasons in American college football, in his familiar tweed fedora, leaning on a golf club watching the girls.

I went over to him and said, "How come an old cod is looking at this young stuff?" He looked at me, cleared his throat and said, "Since I have played with a soft one for so long, I could row a boat with a rope."

Working with some great people

Many country stars came out for Grandpa Jones birthday party. From left are Grandpa, Curly Putnam, George Lindsay, Grandpa's wife, Ralph Emery, Roy Acuff, Gordie, Roy Clark, Roger Miller, Tennessee Ernie Ford and Ricky Skaggs, who just made the picture by a nose!

Gordie Tapp family photo

Brown bears escape into audience

We were doing a show in York, Pennsylvania – the Pennsylvania State Fair. I was master of ceremonies and had some interesting acts to introduce.

One act was Bruin Hilda and her brown bears – Russian brown bears. Another act was Lorena and Rodener, she came out dressed very seductively pulling a cage that had an ape in it, and the ape would escape from the cage and go through the grandstand, swinging on trapezes that were set up throughout the audience.

The ape was actually her husband in an ape's outfit, but you didn't realize that until the act was over. On this particular night the bears caused a lot of problems because one of the bears, a female bear, was in heat. And I guess she wet on the seat of the bicycle and had got the male all excited and he broke away from the bicycle and ran into the audience.

It was my job to get on stage quickly and relieve everybody's fears that these bears are muzzled, but remind them that the bears have big claws, and to be careful. The advice was to just keep your seat and be quiet.

Eventually they sent men up into the crowd with nets and they captured the bear and put him in his cage.

132

Gordie Tapp

All dressed up with Gordie are Ray Downs, Oscar Peterson, Rick Wilkins, Bucky Piccerelli, Gordie, Tommy Hunter, Dinah Christie, Abe Most and Haygood Hardy. In front is the birthday boy on this occasion, Peter Appleyard.

Then I introduced Lorena and Rodener, and they didn't come out and I'm looking for the entrepreneur, the man that runs the show. And I said, "What do we do Stuie?" He said, "We'll have the band play a tune and you go in and change into Cousin Clem and close the show with Cousin Clem." So I did.

And after the show was over I wanted to know what happened to Lorena and Rodener. And Stuie said, "Well, you're not going to believe this, but they wouldn't go on because they thought the bear stole their act."

And you know when you think of it, it would have been anti-climactic for the ape to go climbing through the trapezes and on the platform after the bear had been in the audience.

The bear really did blow their act. That's one of the funny things that can happen to you when you're out there on the stage in show business.

133

Cousin Clem a hick - but he's not stupid!

Cousin Clem knows how to get the audience laughing.

Library and Archives Canada / Gordie Tapp Collection

17

Cousin Clem is a hick
- but he's not stupid!

Cousin Clem is a character that I developed on the *Main Street Jamboree*. We needed a comedy character so I came up with Cousin Clem.

Cousin Clem is a hick, but he's not stupid. He could be made fun of, but he seems to have the upper hand.

It was kind of fun developing the character, I imitated the accent of my relatives who lived in Exeter, Ontario, because people used to say 'I don't hear farmers talking like that,' but they all did. My accent at that time was: 'Hello there Gordie, I knew it was you because of yer car.'

And, of course, as Cousin Clem developed in the U.S. he started to talk with an accent that favoured the southern audience.

Anyway, it was fun writing material for him. Cousin Clem did stuff like, "I shouldn't be here tonight, because we just lost grandma: 'Course it's time for her to go 'cause she was 103. Mom used to say to her 'Where you want to be buried Ma?' And I used to think that was an awful way to talk to somebody that was cramming for their finals. Well, I guess she figured it was time to go, 'cause all she did was lie around on an old sofa in the kitchen sucking on a bottle of Blue Light. And one day she said, 'This bottle of Blue Light is empty. If you open the window, I'll fling it and wherever it lands, that's where you can

Cousin Clem a hick - but he's not stupid!

Cousin Clem gets up close and personal at a milking display. Looking on his radio announcer Paul Reid.

bury me.' And we opened the window, and she flung it. And we buried her on top of the kitchen cupboard.

But she really died of a broken heart. She had a little dog called spot, and that used to confuse the dog 'cause he was black all over. Spot went deaf, and no, there's nothing worse than a deaf dog. 'You want to go for a walk?' It just stands there and looks at ya. So she read in a magazine about a hearing aid for a dog.

Gordie Tapp

She saved up her pension money and she sent and got the hearing aid. And when it arrived I helped her with it – a little button that fit in the dog's ear and a little wire runs down its back with a strap around its tummy, with a battery. And as soon as you put it in, you knew the dog could hear. 'You want to go for a walk?' He went right through the screen door and just left a gaping hole in it. He ran down the lane and he listened, and he heard the grass growing and the birds singing. He even heard the dog barking next door, and it had been dead for two years.

He got so excited and he ran to the end of the lane, cocked his leg up to the tree, went on the battery and electrocuted himself. And that was devastating.

Grandma was a good cook. She used to cook some of the best – she cooked a white bean birthday cake, and boy I tell you people used to say 'A white bean birthday cake? What does it taste like?' I said 'It tasted awfully good, besides, it blowed out its own candles.'

She used to make dill pickles in big crocks. She called me one day and said 'Clem. This crock has got too much alum in it. You got to dump it out for me.' And I said 'You're sure?' 'Yeah' she said, 'I'm sure. Just go dump it out in the yard.' So I took it out and dumped it. And by golly it had a lot of alum in it, 'cause it sucked the outhouse right up onto the back porch."

I mean, it's this kind of material that I've had fun with Clem. Stories like that, stories of Clem and his brother, Orville. Orville wasn't carrying a full pail of cream, let's put it that way. He had a dog that had no legs, and he used to take it out at night for a drag. He used to push the thing around in a wheelbarrow. One night he came in all tuckered out, and I said " Orville, you're tired. What's the matter?" He said "That dang dog of mine got to chasing a rabbit; nearly run the legs off me."

Cousin Clem delivering one of his great stories.

Cousin Clem a hick - but he's not stupid!

I mean that kind of material – it's fun, it doesn't hurt anybody, and we got a lot of laughs with it. Clem and Orville were walking in the woods one day and they came to a big hole. And Orville said 'I wonder how deep it is?' Clem said 'Get a stone and drop it down there.' They did and they listened. They didn't hear anything. 'We need a big boulder,' so they got a big boulder and rolled it over and down into the hole. They listened and didn't hear anything. Clem says 'I think it goes all the way to China, that thing is really deep. We need something big to throw down there.' And Orville says 'There's a railroad tie over there. Grab on the other end of it and we'll chuck it down.' So they did and they listened and they didn't hear anything. All of a sudden a goat came out of the woods and dashed between them and down the hole.

And Orville says "That thing is doing 100 mile an hour. He must have been crazy that goat."

Then some fella came out of the woods and said 'Hey, you boys see a goat up here?'

Clem says, "We saw him all right. He just went between us and down that hole doing 100 mile an hour."

'Ha ha," he said, "That wouldn't be my goat. I had my goat chained to a railroad tie.'

Material that didn't hurt then, never ever hurt anybody, but just was real funny. Yeah, it's not uptown humour, I'll agree with you, but I've heard a lot of uptown humour, and it kind of makes me cry when I hear them using that kind of language. I think you take a lot of chances on an audience. I would rather them say 'He was clean, he didn't work long' than, 'my gosh, He was filthy.'

It's a funny world. I guess, every comic has his own way of doing it. Of course, there are a lot out there who are similar, but I think if you favour your audience, then your audience will favour you. Cousin Clem is a good part of my life.

When we started *Hee Haw*, remember I'm a country boy from south of London, Ontario, I was the head writer for the first couple of years, they gave me the assignment of writing Grandpa's Menus, remember they used to say, "what's for supper Grandpa?" And he'd go through all the stuff.

I said, "I don't know anything about Southern cooking." They said, "Learn."

So every Sunday when we weren't shooting I used to go out into the country and talk to farm women, and it's amazing the things I was able to learn and write down and put into Grandpa's script and really give it a little authenticity.

Gordie Tapp

Cousin Clem belts out one of his ditties.

I was in one place and a the little old lady said, "Would you like a drink?" I said, "Yeah." I thought I was going to get some moonshine because we were way out in the country. She went into the house and she came out with a bowl full of buttermilk.

I sat beside her on the stoop sipping on that buttermilk, which I didn't care that much for and a little pig came over and began to chew on my boot. I said, "He's a friendly little fellow, isn't he?"

She said, "He oughta be, you're drinkin' out of his bowl." Wonderful, wonderful humour, and I found out about it in the southern states.

Cousin Clem a hick - but he's not stupid!

Later I used to tell the story about two old East Tennessee hillbillies that met on the road. The one said, 'Buford, did you get married?' He said, "Well dang, I heard you did. Did you all marry your girl from North Carolina?"

Cousin Clem always smiling.

"No, I married a girl from Kentucky."

"Well you was runnin' with a girl from North Carolina."

"Yes," he says, "I was, but do you know it costs $3 to get married in North Carolina, and it only costs $2 to get married in Kentucky, and my brother slept with them both and said there wasn't a dollar's worth of difference." Now, I don't care what you say, you can't beat that kind of humor.

A lot of these things that happened I incorporated into my act. It lent a kind of southern charm that the people in the south kind of appreciated. It made people in the north smile, thinking that southern folk were that way. I guess it's the same way we smile when we hear things about the people from Newfoundland. What wonderful people, every opportunity I get, I go to that province, just to listen to them and hear their humor.

I remember the first time I walked into the CBC studio in St. John's and I met this man, he looked at me and said, 'bye goll, you're the guy on the TV.' I said, 'that's right, how do you know?' He said, ' 'cause you look like me wife.' I said, 'what about the mustache.' He said, 'you're right, hers is bigger,' and he walked away. I mean, that's humour, and they are that way, wonderful.

Gordie Tapp

The Culhanes (Gordie's on the left) was one of the many *Hee Haw* skits that attracted 50 million viewers every week. The other Culhanes are Junior Samples, Grandpa Jones and Lulu Roman.

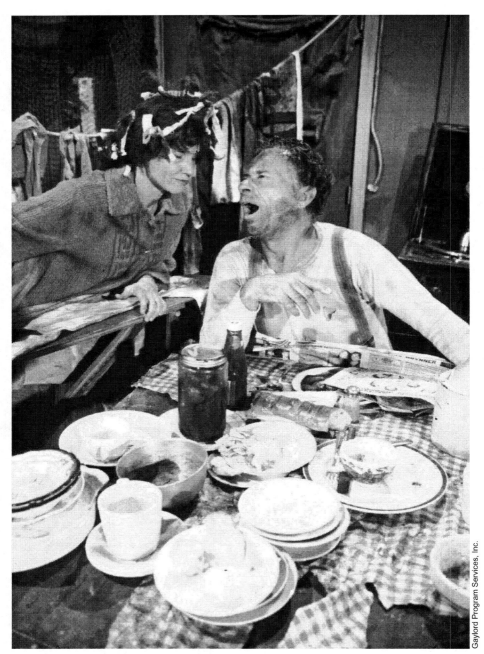

The Naggers on *Hee Haw,* Roni Stoneman and Gordie

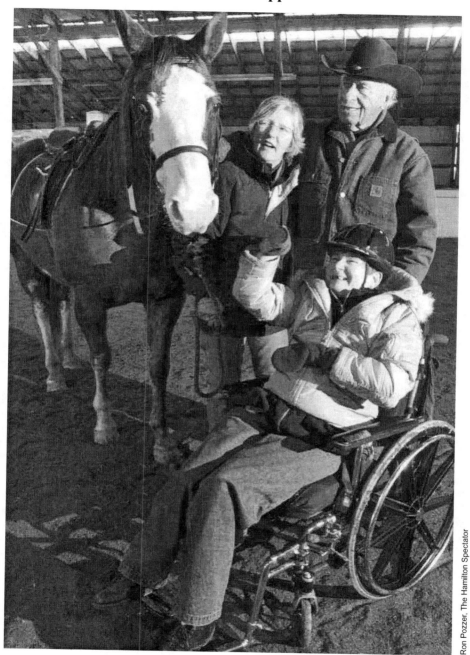

Ron Pozzer, The Hamilton Spectator

When Gordie's 14-year-old horse, Sheri, started going blind in one eye he decided to give her to the Equestrian Association for the Disabled at their Mount Hope stables near Hamilton. With Gordie and Sheri are riding instructor Pat Bullock and Sheri Burns.

Gordie's love for horses

Dismatsek Photo, Hamilton

Gordie loves to be around horses. Here he is with a friend's horse.

18

Gordie's love for horses

Irode horses from the time I was 12 or 13. I have had as many as 31 horses, including boarders, at my farm on Appleby Line. I have always been interested in horses, they can be a great companion.

I guess my love for horses started years ago. My relatives in Exeter used to let me go to stay with them during harvest, and I'd help with the chores. We would ride, and there was a topsie, I remember; a grey. She was a buggy horse that they used to go to town and to church.

We also rode Maud and Bob, they were draught horses that pulled the binder, the disks, and the scuffler, and all the rest of the equipment used on a farm.

I got to like horses in Exeter and over the past 70 years it has grown into a love for these beautiful animals. I still love to ride, even though I am now 84. I just love to be around horses.

As a teenager I got a job working for a man named Tom Ryan. He was an Irishman who had been in the British cavalry and had trained under the very difficult stipulations for riders in the cavalry. My father-in-law was in the cavalry and I remember him telling me that he used to have to ride over jumps sitting backward on a horse leading four other horses.

To do that you have to become a real horseman.

Gordie's love for horses

Library and Archives Canada / Gordie Tapp Collection

Gordie gives a helping hand to his son, Jeffrey, who used to like riding with his dad. All Gordie's daughters share their father's love for horses and used to ride - and show - horses in shows around Ontario.

Tom didn't teach me that cavalry trick, but he did teach me some of the finer points of riding and horsemanship.

He taught me how to sit up straight in the saddle, an English saddle. What he did was have me put a penny - that's when we had pennies that were bigger than the pennies we have today, they were about as big as a 50-cent piece - between each knee and the saddle. I had to squeeze my knees to the saddle,

146

which was difficult enough while standing. Imagine how difficult it was when the horse started moving - and Tom wanted us to canter and to gallop without dropping that penny.

At first I thought he was kidding when he gave me a couple of pennies and told me how he wanted me to use them. But I soon found out he sure wasn't kidding. But it's that little trick that helped make riding so wonderful for me and kept me interested all these years.

One of the jobs he gave me to do was to take his horses to be shod at the blacksmith's. Tom lived behind our place on Baseline Road in London, and his property actually ran alongside ours. It wasn't a long commute when I went to work!

I made 50 cents a week back then and sometimes I'd have lunch while I was working with Tom.

Tom was a great, old character. I remember he smoked a pipe and he used to put the tobacco in his hands before filling his pipe. He'd then run the tobacco through his fingers to make sure all the tobacco got into his pipe.

We lived about 10 miles from Lambeth, where the blacksmith was located. I used to ride the horse there, wait while he was shod, then ride him back. I would do this about every other week.

Back then that was a great ride. You know what it is like when you are young - distance is not a factor. I don't know whether I would want to ride that far today. I don't feel old, but sometimes my bones don't seem to agree with my mind.

Tom was quite a guy. I learned a lot from him about horses.

There's something about having a friendship with a horse. Oh, I guess you can feel that way about a dog, but it really is different with a horse; it's a relationship that you just can't explain. If the horse likes you, it's great.

If the horse doesn't like you, it becomes a bit of a challenge.

I have a mare now that doesn't like men. My daughter can do anything with her, but she stubbornly refuses to listen to me. In fact, the other day she knocked me over and jumped right over me and ran away.

I've had 11 broken bones as a result of being around horses, so I'm kind of

Gordie's love for horses

Gordie rides with one of his daughters, Barbara.

accustomed to them. What a way to become accustomed!

As a young teenager riding those horses 10 miles each way to visit the blacksmith, you can imagine how much I liked that first paying job.

I don't think I ever imagined that I would one day be as lucky as my friend and neighbour, Tom, and have a number of horses of my own.

Getting a saddle just like Carl Smith's

I was working with Carl Smith, who was at the Grand Ole Opry. He was with his wife, June Carter, who later married Johnny Cash.

148

Gordie Tapp

Carl had cutting horses. I used to ride with him and train the horses.

He had a saddle that I liked, I said, "I'd like to get a saddle like that." He said, "Here call Whistle Ryan in Texas and give him your name and tell him what you want." So I called him and said, "Mr. Ryan, I'm a friend of Carl Smith's and I've been riding in his Buster Welch saddle and I'd

Gordie and Helen with Julie Speck, chairperson of Milton District Hospital's fundraising gala called Blazing Saddles in 2005. Gordie was MC for the event.

Halton Compass / Stephen Baker

like one. Do you think if I send you the size of my hips, and my buttocks and the lengths of my legs you can make one and send it to me and if I like it I can send you a cheque?" He said, "Why don't you send us a cheque and if we like it we'll send you a saddle."

It's a true story. He said, "Who the hell are you?" I said, "I'm Gordie Tapp and I'm on a show called *Hee Haw*." "My God, yes, we'll get the saddle ready and send it to you." And they did.

I rode with Carl and used the saddle for a couple of years down there. When I brought it home, I had to bring it in a big box. I came through Customs and the guy said, "Hey, here he is, what do you have this time?" I said, "I've got a saddle."

"Is it used?"

"It is."

"Well, we're going to have to have it appraised."

I said, "Ok, I'll see you later." I started to walk out when he said, "Where are you going?" I said, "If you think I'm sitting around here while you get that thing appraised, forget it." He said, "Get that thing out of here, I'll be filling out forms for two months." I put it on my back and carried it out.

Gordie's love for horses

I was invited during *Country Hoedown* days to be in the parade at the Brandon Fair, in Brandon, Manitoba.

They asked me if I would ride a horse. And I said "Of course. I'm a horseman; I'd love to ride a horse." So they told the boys in the stable "Get a horse for Gordie Tapp." And one of the guys said "You mean the guy on TV?" And they said "Yeah." "We'll get him a horse alright." And they got me a stallion.

He was a very beautiful horse, dark palomino. He was a little difficult going over railroad tracks and things like that during the parade. But more than three-quarters of the way through the parade, the float in front of me broke down and they had to take it out of the parade.

So they wheeled it out when we came to a side street, and they moved the whole parade up, and put me behind two hackney ponies that were pulling a buggy with a lady driving. They were pretty little things, and one of them was in heat. I don't know what goes on in my life, but I'm running into this all the time.

Gordie broke his arm when he slipped on the ice at an arena in Wetaskawin, Alberta. He broke the arm in the same place he had broken it in a horse riding injury just a few months previously. Weatherman Peter Saltzman is with Gordie, along with Bert Pearl of *The Happy Gang*.

Anyway the stallion got very agitated and he was showing his excitement in a way a stallion does. He was all over the road, standing up on his hind legs. I was hitting him between the ears with my fist to keep him down.

There were kids all along each side of the road, and I started to get really worried, so I pulled him up and I jumped off, and I took him to some of the parade officials, and I said "You better take care of this stallion because if he's out here on the road he's going to hurt somebody and I'm going to be responsible. They took the horse away and I got in a convertible to finish the parade and wave to the people along the parade route.

Gordie rode this dark palomino in the Brandon parade before it got a little agitated.

Canada's highest award presented to Gordie

Reprinted with the permission of Rideau Hall

Gordie receives the Order of Canada medal from the Governor General of Canada Romeo LeBlanc.

19

Canada's highest award presented to Gordie

I have received the highest civilian honours from my country and my province. Being made an Order of Canada member in the Queen's Honours list in 1998 was a special thrill for me. I have also been awarded the Order of Ontario.

I think when you start anything, you never go seeking praise and awards. I didn't.

I simply was blessed to be in the right place at the right time and never sat back and admired what I had accomplished. The golden spoon was never handed to me in life. When opportunities came my way I was always willing to do what it takes to get the job done.

I had a chance to stop and reflect on my life only after it was announced that I had been nominated to receive the honour. There is usually a time lapse of several months between the Queen's announcement and going to Rideau Hall in Ottawa - the home of the Governor General of Canada, the Queen's representative in Canada - and receiving the Order of Canada award.

It is a humbling experience to be recognized by your country in this way. The tendency is to believe that you only did what was before you to do - what others invited you to do. In my case the honour came, I believe, not for all my many years as an entertainer, but for things that I did because I was an entertainer.

Canada's highest award presented to Gordie

Avec les hommages de Leurs Excellences
le très honorable Roméo LeBlanc
Gouverneur général du Canada
et Madame Diana Fowler LeBlanc

With the compliments of Their Excellencies
The Right Honourable Roméo LeBlanc
Governor General of Canada
and Mrs. Diana Fowler LeBlanc

Canada's Governor General Romeo LeBlanc and his wife, Diana, in the middle, with Gordie and his wife Helen at Rideau Hall for the Order of Canada ceremony.

Gordie Tapp

When you are a well-known figure, a personality if you will, groups see you as an opportunity to help them with their cause. I don't want to sound too blunt here, but I just want to lay out my thoughts.

When you are recognizable, of course, automobile makers, toothpaste makers, fast-food chains, running shoe manufacturers all think they can improve their bottom line by getting someone that everyone knows to be their spokesperson or marketing icon. For instance, if Tiger Woods gets millions of dollars a year just for lending his name to a golf product, the manufacturer, Tiger, and the public all win. We, the public, think that if Tiger's marketing the product - and using it - it must be good, see how well he plays. I'll buy that and maybe I'll play better than I do now, maybe even as good as Tiger.

In a similar vein, charitable organizations use the same thinking in their marketing decisions. If they can get a prominent figure, they feel it will be easier to attain their goals.

I was lucky enough to be chosen to be the chairman for many years for the Canadian muscular dystrophy campaign, and I also helped the U.S. Shriners' hospitals, particularly on their children's campaigns, and the Tim Horton Foundation for children in Canada, which, among other things, makes sure that underprivileged children get a chance to go to summer camp.

I was particularly grateful to be able to do my part, such as it was, to help these organizations. I don't mean to downplay my involvement, but I don't think I was the only person who was capable of doing what I was doing for them. This, of course, is where being in the right place at the right time comes into play.

As a member of the *Hee Haw* cast it gave me that opportunity for others to benefit in a very real way from my 15 minutes of fame, so to speak.

I think I said at the time that the laughter Cousin Clem provoked was great medicine for millions of Canadians and Americans who used to tune in to see *Hee Haw* for more than 25 years.

But the fund-raising for hospitals and medical research probably helped the country to be a better place. Please forgive me if that sounds a little egotistical. I don't mean it to be that way, I just want to point out that this is the way that personalities have a chance to give back to society - doing charitable work is better than simply cutting a cheque for an organization and moving on with your life.

Canada's highest award presented to Gordie

OFFICE OF
THE LIEUTENANT GOVERNOR
QUEEN'S PARK
TORONTO, ONTARIO
M7A 1A1

TEL. (416) 325-7780
FAX (416) 325-7787

August 13, 1999

Dear Mr. Tapp:

I am pleased to extend sincere congratulations to you on your appointment to the Order of Ontario.

You have rendered service of the greatest distinction and of singular excellence to the benefit of society in Ontario and elsewhere.

As The Queen's representative in this province and as Honorary Chairman of the Advisory Council, it will be my pleasure to formally welcome you to membership in the Order of Ontario at your investiture on Monday, October 25, 1999.

Sincerely,

Hilary M. Weston
Lieutenant Governor

Mr. Gordie Tapp, CM, OOnt
4211-7 Millcroft Drive
Burlington, Ontario
L7M 3Y9

Gordie was appointed to the Order of Ontario in 1999.

Gordie Tapp

I think many personalities could write a cheque from their bank accounts to give an organization the money they need to continue to operate. Even if that cheque was more than the total money raised during the length of the campaign, it's better to be the figurehead and be seen to be doing something worthwhile. It plants seeds in people's minds - and the donation they make this year often turns into a donation every year for a lifetime.

I learned a lot from my charity work - and I cherish the special moments that I became privy to, especially when I was introduced to those children and adults who benefited most from the money raised in the campaigns I was lucky to be associated with over the years.

I have a friend who has muscular dystrophy and it breaks my heart to see them suffer. I often think 'why them and not me?' But, of course, that just tugs at the heartstrings and makes you want to do more. If I become incapacitated how would I cope? I hope there would be someone who would be my care-giver, my advocate, someone who has the capacity to help not only the one, but the hundreds, thousands, maybe millions, who currently suffer. Maybe their caring now - their devotion of time and talent may help the generations to come that may not have to suffer as much as those today.

I have learned a lot about how people cope with disease and hardships during my years of being privileged to work in medical charity work.

I feel good about my attachment to these charities over the years. Could I have done more? I am sure we all have the benefit of looking in that rear-view mirror and saying that with a little more effort, a little more juggling of schedules, a little more sacrifice - perhaps being away from home more, perhaps choosing a charity performance over a paid performance - maybe, just maybe, we could have made an even bigger difference.

You get the message, I'm sure. We should all take time to help those less fortunate whenever we can.

When you raise money for medical research, you know it is going to the right place. When you raise money for children who can't raise money for themselves it gives you a felling inside that is hard to describe, other than it is warm and it makes you feel good, knowing that the small sacrifices you are making are making some little boy or girl feel better.

After I received the Order of Canada I was told by my provincial member of parliament, my MPP, that I was going to receive the Order of Ontario. I was quite thrilled about it.

Canada's highest award presented to Gordie

However, when the list came out and my name wasn't on it I wondered why. Naturally, I was a little disappointed.

A little while later. I was playing golf with the Premier of Ontario, Mike Harris, and during our golf game he said "Gordie, I'm really very sorry about the Order of Ontario. I thought for sure you were going to receive it. I have no control over the committee that makes the decisions. But I wanted you to know how I felt." I said "Well, that's all right Mike, after all I got the big one." He laughed, and we're still friends, I hope.

In due course I was awarded the Order of Ontario and again, the same feelings that overwhelmed me when I was at Rideau Hall in Ottawa, returned for

Gordie with Ontario Lieutenant Governor Hilary Weston at his investiture into the Order of Ontario.

Library and Archives Canada / Gordie Tapp Collection

the special ceremonies with Ontario's Lieutenant Governor, Hilary Weston, a charming lady and a credit to our province.

Gordie Tapp

Gordon Tapp
1999 Recipient of The Order of Ontario

It's not every day that a Canadian is recognized as one of the world's funniest storytellers by the president of the United States. This, however, can be said of Gordie Tapp, a Burlington resident and a radio and television icon in Canada. It was former U.S. president Gerald Ford who once described Mr. Tapp that way, and it is safe to say many people would have agreed. A talent and penchant for entertaining people was evident at an early age, as Mr. Tapp was a five-year-old member of the O'Dell School Harmonica Band south of London. After joining the army in 1942, he won the Canadian Army Amateur Contest. This opened up a new door of opportunity for Mr. Tapp - entertaining the troops. Between the 1950s and 1970s, he played every military base in Canada and embarked on 27 tours around the world for members of the Canadian Armed Forces, their families and the Diplomatic Corps. Amidst all of Mr. Tapp's accomplishments, perhaps the most famous of all was his idea to start up a new type of variety show in 1969 that would mix his kind of music and humour. The show, of course, was Hee Haw. In the 1950s and 60s Mr. Tapp was a fixture on CBC Radio and TV - and is well remembered for his long running Main Street Jamboree and Country Hoedown programs. His reputation as a great entertainer and host led to his serving as the MC of Canada's Centennial party on Parliament Hill in 1967. Mr. Tapp's eager willingness to raise funds for charity is also well known. His efforts helped raise hundreds of thousands of dollars for Shriner's hospitals. Mr. Tapp has earned many awards over the years - not only as an entertainer with staying power, but for always being ready to support worthy causes.

I am very thankful for both these honours. They are an extra-special 'thank-you' not only from our political leaders, but from all those involved with the organizations I have had the privilege to work with and the beautiful people - especially the children - who make charitable work such a blessing. I am proud to be associated with you all.

Canada's highest award presented to Gordie

F1

Section editor Philip Bast
894-2231, ext. 630

Kitchener-Waterloo Record

Wednesday, June 6, 1990

Enterta

Gordon Lightfoot (top left) and Roy Clark (bottom left) are among the country stars paying tribute to Gordie Tapp (above, with Tommy Hunter looking over his shoulder) Tuesday at Centre in the Square.

The Kitchener-Waterloo Record did Gordie proud . . .

inment

Inside

The Guelph Spring Festival is looking forward to the opening of a new civic arts centre. Page F2

Lordy be, what a show!

Cornpone tribute to Gordie Tapp makes for a mighty fine evening

By John Greenwood
Special to The Record

Two huge caricatures grinned down on a full house at the Centre in the Square Tuesday night. Each was the smilin' face of Cousin Clem, the cornpone comic alter ego of Gordie Tapp, who was celebrating 50 years in show business with some of his longtime friends.

By golly, it was a down home kinda night, don't ya know, where the stories and memories were as good as the music.

'Course, when he first heard about the idea, ol' Gordie wasn't sure just how many of his friends would show up. But show up they did, to sing and play, to joke and reminisce.

Gosh, the MC was Canada's Country Gentleman himself, Tommy Hunter, eight feet tall and 85 years on CBC. He's an awfully nice fella, Tommy is, real sincere. He sang Talk About the Good Times, and his Number One Country Hit — 'cause if ya stay around long enough you can git a No. 1 country hit — The Man of '87.

He and Gordie go back to Country Hoedown together, and the days of live TV.

As does another Gordie paying tribute, Gordie Lightfoot. He was one of the Singin' Swingin' Eight, a square dance group on the old Hoedown show. He used to alla-man-left when he was supposed to do-si-do. They called him Gordon Leadfoot.

'Course, Gordon's gone on to better things. Boy, has he ever, sellin' millions o' records world wide, the favorite son of Orillia. He played a couple o' real intimate ballads, the kind of breathless thing he's known for. He said he especially enjoyed the camaraderie on the old show.

Then there was Canada's Maritime Sweetheart with the Voice of an Angel, Catherine McKinnon. She remembers doin' Armed Forces shows with Gordie. She was taller back then, she says, "and God knows I was thinner!" She was born to sing Nova Scotia Farewell, bein' from there an' all, and sing it she did. Her high,

ron's more famous self, Charlie Farquharson. Charlie said Gordie Tapp was the only man what could keep this country together, what with Blarney Bullroney and the premiers makin' a mess of things.

Charlie and Gordie have been together for years on Hee Haw, what Charlie calls America's Sesame Street for Grown Ups. Charlie says Gordie can do his bit for national unity by goin' to Quebec and speakin' French, after Quebecers hear his French, they'll speak English in self-defence!

Another Hee Haw buddy, 87 years old and goin' strong, Louis Marshall "Grandpa" Jones was there too. Lordy be, he kin make a teenager feel old the way he plays Banjo Man on that ol' banjo o' his.

And Roy Clark, Hee Haw's original host, and still hosting after 22 years on that show, was there too. He's won more awards than you can shake a stick at, and he plays a real mean guitar, Roy does. He played Hey Good Lookin' ("how's 'bout cookin' somethin' up with me?"), his famous Yesterday When I Was Young, and his feeverish and stunning Spanish tune Malaguena.

He remembers seein' Gordie on Canadian TV back in '64 or '65. Seems Gordie was doin' a live comic bit with a pig that night. And the pig hadn't ... before the show ... evidently not. So it did it on the stage. Right there on live TV. And he found out later from Gordie himself that Gordie was "the guy with the pig!"

Peter Appleyard played too, Canada's Gentleman of Jazz. He did NATO tours with Gordie, way back when. Peter played eight years with living legend Benny Goodman, so the medley of Goodman tunes Peter did on the vibraphone was mighty fine.

Then he did his own P.E.I Polka, where the audience gets to clap along — and gets to try the coda three times to get it right.

Then, just before intermission, Mr. Appleyard took Sweet Georgia Brown (the tune, not the girl) out for a spin. Spin, heck, he took it out the way you take out an ol' Dodge pick up on a country road to see what she'll do. On the same tune he played vibes, piano, and drums, all

. . . on the occasion of his 50th anniversary in show business.

Canada's highest award presented to Gordie

May 21, 1990

My Dear Gordy,

I am so happy for you, and the great tribute being paid to you. You are so deserving.

I'm sad for me, that I couldn't be there with you, tho I wanted to, so very, very, much; but I am getting a bionic knee, and I just couldn't travel, it would be too difficult.

I was listening to an air check, of of your first appearance on my T.V. show, and I surprised you dressed up in your cousin Clem outfit, do you remember? You were actually short for words; it was a hoot.

I also found some pictures of our trip to Resolute Bay, and the last time I saw you, at the Telethon in Winnipeg.

I have all these wonderful memories of you, as all your fans have.

I was going to sing "For The Good Times" for you. Pretend I did, okay.

I love you,
Juliette

Juliette belts out a number with Wally Koster and Gordie. She could not make it to the 50th anniversary show in Kitchener, but sent along this letter.

My Dear Gordy,

I am so happy for you, and the great tribute being paid to you. You are so deserving.

I'm sad for me, that I couldn't be there with you, tho I wanted to, so very, very, much, but I am getting a bionic knee, and I just couldn't travel, it would be too difficult.

I was listening to an air check, of your first appearance on my T.V. show, and I was surprised you dressed up in your Cousin Clem outfit, do you remember? You were actually short for words, it was a hoot.

I also found some pictures of our trip to Resolute Bay, and the last time I saw you, at the Telethon in Winnipeg.

I have all these wonderful memories of you, as all your fans have.

I was going to sing "For The Good Times" for you. Pretend I did, okay.

I Love You,

Juliette

Cousin Clem with Juliette - and a typed version of her hand-written note on the previous page.

Canada's highest award presented to Gordie

ANNE MURRAY

Dear Gordie,
Fifty years in showbiz !?!
Now that's a strong stomach !
Congratulations and love,
Anne Murray
+
Bill Langstroth

Anne Murray sends along her congratulations . . .

June 5, 1990

Centre In The Square Theatre
Kitchener, Ontario

Dear Gordie:

Congratulations on your 50th Anniversary in Show Business. You
older performers are an inspiration to us.

Johnny Wayne
Johnny Wayne

Frank Shuster
Frank Shuster

Wayne and Shuster crack a joke with their congratulations - what else would you expect?

Ontario

The Premier	Le Premier ministre	Legislative Building	Hôtel du gouvernemen
of Ontario	de l'Ontario	Queen's Park	Queen's Park
		Toronto, Ontario	Toronto (Ontario)
		M7A 1A1	M7A 1A1

May 1993

Mr. Gordon Tapp
4211-7 Millcroft Drive
Burlington, Ontario
L7M 3Y9

Dear 'Tapper':

Please accept my best wishes on the celebration of your 53rd anniversary as entertainer and performer.

Your career, from the early days in radio, to nightclub acts and your television fame on Country Hoedown and as Cousin Clem on Hee Haw, has made you a Canadian institution. Your talents have been enjoyed and appreciated by audiences far and wide making you a worthy ambassador of this country.

I'm delighted to see that the Royal Bank is giving yet another generation of admirers the opportunity to appreciate your enormous skills. This recognition is fitting for a truly Canadian professional.

Yours sincerely,

Bob Rae

Ontario Premier Bob Rae calls Gordie 'a worthy ambassador of this country'

Canada's highest award presented to Gordie

Saskatchewan's Lieutenant Governor Dr. Lynda Haverstock surprised Gordie with the Saskatchewan medal when he was doing one of his many shows in that province. The presentation was in recognition of his many performances throughout Saskatchewan.

166

Gordie Tapp

Gordie was presented with this painting of himself and Cousin Clem.

Gordie and Juliette visit a young patient in the Moose Factory hospital.

The Naggers in familiar surroundings on *Hee Haw* - Roni Stoneman and Gordie.

20

If I have a regret -
it's I didn't stay in LA

I feel pretty good about my life, and let me put it this way, I accomplished most of the things I wanted to accomplish. I would have liked to have done more movies than the three I did. I didn't do enough to get to the position where I could really express myself and be myself, but I'm very satisfied with my achievements.

I think what I regret most is that I didn't stay in Los Angeles and do the things that I would have done, had I been there. The opportunities were all around me, but I had my wife and family in Canada. I felt I had to keep coming back there and keep my base, and I guess that's what kept my feet on the ground.

I'm amused by the very fact that although I wanted to be one of the best comics in the world, I'm not hammy. I can't stand hammy performers, guys who do pratfalls, without mentioning any names, I'm sure you know a number that do that sort of thing. That to me, doing slapstick, sent chills up my spine.

I would much rather take a very difficult story, put a dialect to it and tell it so that I have rapt attention when I'm working on it.

I'm very thankful for the people I've met in the business and the people who've given me the opportunity to be myself and do what I do and encourage me.

Norman Jewison, who went on to become one of the most recognized movie

If I have a regret - it's I didn't stay in LA

producers and directors of the 20th century - and he is still making big box-office successes in 2006 - came and did *Country Hoedown* for a few weeks in the 1950s. He also directed the *Wayne and Shuster* TV series for CBC in 1954 after graduation from the University of Toronto. It wasn't long before he was director and producer of the *Judy Garland Show* for U.S. television, working with Judy, Frank Sinatra and Dean Martin.

It wasn't difficult for me to see why Norman made a reputation for himself so quickly. He was a wonderful guy to work with - he just had a way of telling you to throw away the script and be yourself. If you didn't know the lines, he'd tell you to pick up the script and then do it the way you would do it if it was just coming off the top of your head.

There are other producers and directors who I worked with who got very angry. But they don't get the same kind of results that way. They make you feel uncomfortable with them.

I've worked with some great people, Sam Lovullo from *Hee Haw,* who had been with CBS before he came to us, just a marvelous man to work for, he'd say, "what do you think about this?" Not, "do it this way." That makes a great difference in the way you perform and the way you get on in life.

One thing that ruffles me - and it always has - is when someone is angry with me. It really bothers me.

I want to reconcile things immediately and get it straightened out and make them understand that I'm sorry that it was my mistake. I can't stand things being allowed to fester.

I work with a lot of people that don't care about each other's feelings, and it really does bother me if I'm working in an audience and I see somebody get up and leave, I wonder, 'What did I say? What have I done? Why are they not staying?' That bothers you when you're working, because it upsets your rhythm, it upsets your thinking, because when you start thinking about why somebody didn't like what you did, you're not thinking about what you're doing, so it was very important to me to have people like me.

I don't think that's a bad thing, but sometimes it can get in the way.

I lived in Sarasota, Florida for some time, we had a place there for 20 years where I had my fishing boat at the back door. I miss that, I really do miss that, although we have a boat now up here on Lake Erie, and I have it with my son, I miss my diesel fishing boat. I had a lot of fun with it, it was a sports

Gordie Tapp

fisherman. I got a 148 ½-pound blue marlin from this boat, as well as a couple of other good-sized fish, including a 100-pound tarpon. The marlin is on my wall downstairs. I wasn't proud of it, but he was too badly hurt and we couldn't turn him loose. I never felt remorse like I felt when he came into the boat. He was so beautiful, so blue and silver, but within 20 minutes he was a dead lead grey. I thought, gosh this thing's as big as I am, did I have the right?

I have carried on fishing, but I now use the catch and release method. I don't keep them, no matter how big they are.

I caught a 100-pound tarpon in Boca Grand, and we just brought him alongside of the boat, weighed him and turned him loose. It's also very costly to have them mounted, but that wasn't the main reason. My wife said that she didn't want to have to dust it any more. She was right about that.

Living down there in Sarasota was called Clown City or Circus City, and at that time it was the headquarters for Ringling Brothers. We used to see all kinds of circus people. I used to tell the joke that my neighbour was a trapeze artist, and he caught his wife in the act. But seriously, we used to see circus people regularly. I remember one day, we were in the mall, there were some children looking at a display of rattlesnakes encased in plastic. This man had them as paperweights. He had also made lamps out of them. I almost spoke to the kids to tell them to leave them alone when I realized they weren't children, they were midgets. They lived in the area I suppose.

A man who lived quite close to us, before he left this world was Emmett Kelly, one of the world's most renowned clowns.

His daughter told a wonderful story, and I thought it was typical of a circus person.

They had a cat, and everybody vied for the cat's attention. She said that when daddy was home, the cat wouldn't pay attention to anybody else but him. She said we could never figure that out, until we noticed that daddy kept a dead shrimp in the cuff of his pants. If you stop and think about it, I worked with dog acts, and when they want the dogs to follow them, they would have wieners in the cuffs of their pants and the dogs would never leave them. Wonderful humor in the world, I wonder if there's enough of it?

In 1968 I travelled up the west coast of the United States and into Canada with an Oriental Review. You talk about humour and the different ways it comes out, and every nationality having their own.

We had, I think, eight Japanese girls and seven Chinese girls on the show, and we had so much fun with them. We were in a club in Seattle and a girl came on stage. She was really quite good. She danced and sang and we all watched. I said to Annie Morimoto, "Is it true that Kyori used to be a booking agent in Nagasaki?" She said 'yes', so I turned to Kyori and said, "what do you think of this performer?"

She said, "She like Charlie McQueen."

I said, "Who?"

"Charlie McQueen."

I turned to Annie and I said, "Who on earth is Charlie McQueen?"

"Ah, she mean Shirley MacLaine."

This girl gave me a lot of laughs. She told me a story, about Japanese people always being polite, they're always bowing, and, of course, you know that if you've watched the movies or if you've been there or if you're associated with Japanese people, they are very, very polite, and they bow a lot.

She said this Japanese couple got married, and after a year it was obvious there was to be an increase in the family, but two years went by and nothing happened and the husband got worried and took her to a specialist in Switzerland who put a large scope on the young lady's abdomen and peered in. And there were two little old men with beards, one saying, "Affer you," and the other saying, "No, affer you."

She cried laughing telling it. I thought, you don't think of Japanese people as having a sense of humour, but that's a sense of humour.

I remember one time doing a convention, I believe it was at the King Eddy (King Edward Hotel, downtown Toronto) at the time, for the Ontario Bar Association. A young man I grew up with, who was my lawyer at the time, was in the audience and I pointed him out. I mentioned that we had grown up together, saying, "You know how when you're a kid, you have plans of what you want to be . . . I always wanted to be an entertainer and he always wanted to be a pirate."

It's funny how he made it and I didn't. I can remember him giving me the finger, but I explained it, in his office he had a picture of a cow with the defendant pulling on the horns and the complainant pulling on the tail and him

GORDIE'S 50th ANNIVERSARY DATE

JUNE 5, 1990

WITH SINCERE APPRECIATION IN RECOGNITION OF YOUR EVERLASTING CONTRIBUTION TO THE SUCCESS OF THE **HEE HAW** SERIES NOW IN ITS 23ᴿᴰ BROADCAST SEASON. IN THE EYES OF MILLIONS WHO HAVE WATCHED YOU PERFORM YOU ARE A "HALL OF FAMER".

HEE HAW CAST, STAFF &CREW
SAM LOVULLO
PRODUCER

Here's the special card sent to Gordie on his 50th anniversary in show business.

on the stool in the middle milking it.

There are so many stories about lawyers, one said to me one time, "You can always tell when a lawyer is lying because his lips are moving." I always tell about my friend the lawyer that I went to with a DUI (driving under the influence) and asked him if he could get it reduced. He did - he got it down to manslaughter.

And then there's the guy who said, "They got me a suspended sentence, they hung me."

There are a lot of good lawyer jokes. A lot of them I can't mention here.

If I have a regret - it's I didn't stay in LA

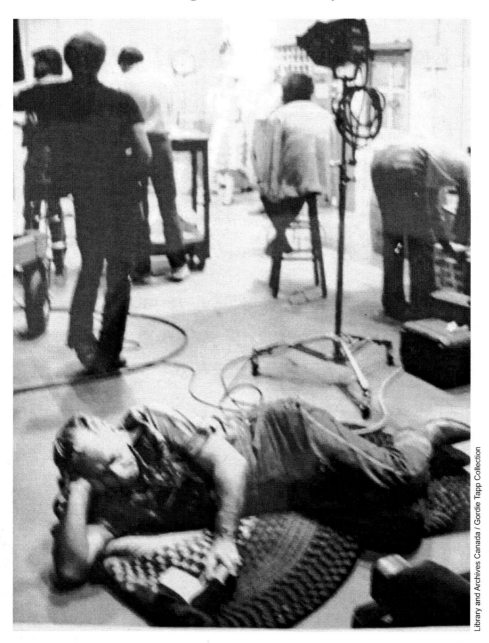

Gordie loves to read . . . and there was plenty of time between 'takes' to get into a book.

Gordie Tapp

Gordie in a familiar pose in *Hee Haw's* general store.

Five of us wrote for Hee Haw

Listening intently as they take direction from the *Hee Haw* booth in Kornfield Kounty are Archie Campbell, Grandpa Jones and Gordie.

21

Five of us wrote for *Hee Haw*

*H*ee Haw's format, as far as building the shows, was done weeks and weeks in advance. There were five of us writers, and each contributed to a certain part of the show.

I was responsible for all of The Naggers with Roni Stoneman and myself at the breakfast table, most of The Storekeeper, where I was the Storekeeper. And I wrote a lot of the Old Philosopher stuff, such as walking out in front of the camera and saying, "A horse can be driven to water, but a pencil must be lead." Then Frank Peppiat would hit my hat and it would fly in the air and my hair would stand up. That's an interesting story about that hair, I'll throw it in here.

Charles was a British makeup man working in Hollywood, who came to work with us on *Hee Haw*. He did a lot of the old historical novels that were made in Britain and was familiar with all the dress and the style of the times. A very interesting man to talk to. When I first went out to Hollywood I had to go see Charles at the makeup studios at CBS. He was arranging for this wig that I was supposed to wear as the Old Philosopher. It was the same wig used by Bing Crosby in *A Yankee in King Arthur's Court*. It was a white wig. Charles had to put it on my head, make it sit securely, cut it so it looked right, but still have

Five of us wrote for Hee Haw

enough hair to twist and turn up when they hit it with the rubber chicken.

He was working on this one morning and he said, 'can you excuse me for a few minutes Gordie? I have to do Gig Young's makeup, he's playing the *Carol Lawrence Show*, and I've got to do it right away.' I said, 'no problem Charles, I'll go and wait outside.'

I went into the hallway and there was a drinking fountain. I walked over to the fountain, and when I arrived there was a white-haired man drinking. When he looked up it was Red Skelton. I said, "Hello Red." He said, "Who the hell are you?"

Years later, we talked, and laughed about the incident. He really was a delightful man, no doubt.

Hee Haw was done in an unusual way which the techies called 'cartoon style.' We would write 13 segments for The Naggers, and then we'd record them all at the same time, so we didn't have to keep changing sets. We would probably do the whole 13 all in one morning.

Now, we never rehearsed anything on *Hee Haw*. You had a script. You learned your lines. They had cue cards, and there were five cameras.

The cue cards were there and always ready, but rarely used. You knew your lines and you felt free working with the people we worked with, because we worked together for so long.

You must remember in 1969, those ladies were beautiful young ladies, in 10 years they were like our sisters and we used to ignore them. It was interesting. Our wardrobe was behind the girls makeup room, I used to open the door and go on through and say, 'close your eyes girls, I'm coming through.' We had a lot of fun, they were gorgeous girls. They were a treat to work with, each in their own way.

I was talking to our producer Sam Lovullo the other day, and he told me about Lulu Roman, you remember Lulu was the big, heavyset girl. She sang *Amazing Grace* at Buck Owens' funeral, and Sam said, he had never seen nor heard such a long, standing ovation. There's still a lot of talent there, and I'm glad it's getting out so that people can know it and appreciate it.

Coincidentally, over a million DVD copies of the *Hee Haw* series that Time Warner put out have been sold. There's still a great demand for *Hee Haw*. It means that people are seeing us again as we were then. I look at it and see all of

Gordie was surprised to find a number of *Hee Haw* magazines at a book store in England

179

Five of us wrote for Hee Haw

Gordie was on the cover of many of the *Hee Haw* magazines he picked up in London, England

my beautiful brown wavy hair. Now it's all white, but it's still waving though, and not waving goodbye, which is a good thing.

It was interesting to do *Hee Haw*, because you almost knew what was going to happen before it happened. I knew that when I worked with Roni, and she was my wife, I used to make her so mad before we went on set that she was ready to kill me, and it showed in her actions. When she hit me with her rolling pin, she meant it. Mind you, the rolling pin was made of leather, but I knew she was hitting me, I'll tell you that.

The Naggers, Roni Stoneman and Gordie in a quieter moment.

Gordie Tapp

Gordie contemplating as The Old Philosopher

Not only was Gordie on the cover . . . his characters were very prominent inside the comic books.

This is the type of humour that had 50 million viewers tune in to *Hee Haw* every week.

22

Minnie Pearl - a real gem

One of the biggest stars I worked with in the country music field was Minnie Pearl. Wonderful lady.

Her husband had a plane and they flew everywhere for her to do shows, and her 'Howdy!' (you'll remember her shrill 'H-o-w---d-e-e-e-e!') became familiar to every country music star, and entertainer, and audience, believe me.

I always took jokes to Minnie Pearl when things happened that I thought she could use. For instance, I was writing grandpa's menus, which was very difficult for me because everything was a southern menu, and I had been born and raised in Westminster Township in London, Ontario in Canada, where beans and wieners were the big thing, and corn flakes.

Anyway, I was talking to this little old lady. She was shelling peas in her skirt and throwing them in a copper kettle. I asked her, 'What do you have on special occasions?'

She said 'We don't have special occasions.'

I said 'No, you misunderstood me. What would you serve your family, say, at Thanksgiving?'

'Country ham.'

Minnie Pearl - a real gem

Gordie trying to give Minnie Pearl a run for her money in the fancy dress stakes.

'Always country ham?'

'Mostly,' she said "once a lady gave me a turkey, but I didn't know how to fix it, so I just cut it up and made chicken and dumplings out of it." And I thought that was so real, and I remember taking it to Minnie and she said 'Oh my dear, isn't that honest. I'll use that,' and I'm sure she did.

One particular thing about Minnie Pearl, I remember we would be working and there'd be a pause and we had to wait until they did a reset or something. And she'd look at you and she'd sing *Have I told you lately that I love you?* We kidded a lot, I'll tell you.

I wrote a joke for her that she got a great kick out of and we used it on *Hee Haw*. I said 'Minnie Pearl is the only woman in television that had a price on her head.' And if you remember, she had a price tag hung on that hat. And why someone hadn't come up with that before me I don't know, but I thought it was good and it was used many times. Minnie Pearl: a great star, and surely, one missed.

Minnie Pearl with the familiar price-tag on the ever-present hat with Gordie on the CBC *Country Hoedown* show

Gordie Tapp

Archie Campbell and Gordie in the middle of the Kornfield

23

How to really tell a story

To tell a story, first you must know your audience. There's no sense in telling a bank joke to a blacksmith. Also, if you use an accent, make sure that you know the accent. Don't tell a story that's four miles long when it can be told in a mile-and-a-half.

The shorter you tell the story and get to the punch line, the better. Timing is also most essential. When you get to the punch line, you want to wait just a moment! Then hit them with it.

It's all those little things that make a story realistic, understandable and authentic.

You really have to think when you're telling stories, if you do that you will maintain your audience.

I'm telling stories these days mostly to seniors. Being a senior myself, we have a lot of shared feelings . . . I don't think there's anything more rewarding than hearing seniors laugh.

I have always had a knack for remembering jokes. I can resurrect one from memory in a moment to respond to a comment or a situation.

I don't have to write jokes any more. It's a gift for sure, although I really worked at it in the early years when I was in radio. I think the talent is not only

How to really tell a story

in the presentation, the story-telling part, but it is in the ability to be able to cater a joke to your audience – based on their profession, their ethnicity, their politics, or their shared interest, such as cooking, or golf, or undertakers.

Yes, I even spoke at a convention for undertakers in London, Ontario. We did the show at a London hotel and every casket maker in the business had their products there and there were all kinds – small caskets for babies and children, large caskets for grown ups, and some extremely large caskets for big people.

I think that undertakers are the craziest guys in the world, to tell you the truth. It was amazing, because every time you'd go to look at a casket they'd have somebody lying in it. Probably one of the workers or one of the undertakers themselves. You'd go along and you'd stand there looking at the casket and the body, and then they'd wink at you. I tell you it came as a surprise, I didn't realize that that's what they were doing, putting their own people in.

But they're a bunch of characters, they raised eyebrows that night and I'll never forget it.

Here's a wonderful story, relative to the undertaker. Well, it's a bit naughty, but it's funny:

This elderly lady went to the undertaker's parlour to see a friend who'd passed away. And on her way out, she's met by the undertaker who says "You knew Mrs. Palmer?"

"Oh yes," she said "I knew her well. We were friends for many, many years. She's 92, you know."

"Yes," said the undertaker, "I knew she was 92. By the way, how old are you?"

And she said, "Ninety-eight."

The undertaker responded, "Ninety-eight? It's hardly worth going home, is it?"

I don't think anyone can tell you that they have an original joke. They are all based on a story told by someone else. Many would call it theft, but I like to think of it as research.

Few jokes I hear I retell the same way, that's why I call it research, rather than theft. I change the character to fit my situation or I use the punch line on a story I am already telling . . . but now there is a better punch line.

Gordie and Archie Campbell in *Hee Haw's* skit *Pfft you was gone.*

Gaylord Program Services, Inc.

On *Hee Haw* we had to be careful about the kind of humour we wrote because we were working to the Bible belt. I don't think you need to be a rocket-scientist to figure out that an off-colour joke could turn off a huge part of

How to really tell a story

your audience. We went close to the bone every show, but we knew where the line was drawn. We never crossed it. That's why we were welcomed into 50 million homes every week. Don't think it was easy not to offend one of those 50 million. It was on our minds. And we used to come up with some punch lines that made us laugh and would have made millions laugh . . . but we chose the less offensive one for the show.

That ability to respect our audience, rather than to blast away claiming artistic expression gave all of us a*t Hee Haw* a nice, long run. Not often do you get a chance in show business to talk to several generations at once . . and continue to be telling jokes to your original audience's children . . and then even their children.

I don't want to leave the impression that we never got complaints about our material. I remember one about a little girl with a wooden leg. We got a complaint from a paraplegic society.

Stuff like this got through. It probably shouldn't, but it did. And we all learned more about our audience.

I think a lot of humour hurts someone. But to prevent being hurt you have to be able to laugh at yourself. I think that's the key. If you can see the funny side of the way you dress, the way you talk, the expressions you have, that helps you to laugh at yourself, or your people. Knowing that the intent was not to be mean or spiteful, but simply to overplay a trait, or highlight something special about you or your people.

Maybe our mainly rural audience was more forgiving than others, but I know they used to love to laugh at themselves.

I do a lot of dialect story-telling. That involves a lot of English, Irish, Scottish, Jewish, Polish and Newfoundlander lingo and the rural Southern U.S. twang.

About the closest I ever came to someone taking me to task over some of my material was in the Hamilton Spectator - my hometown daily, in fact. Funny how things work that way isn't it? You can tell stories all over the world, get home and tell the same stories and someone takes you to task. And this one, they didn't let it go. The story was dragged on for about a week.

I had been the Master of Ceremonies at a event to pay tribute to the retiring mayor of Burlington, Walter Mulkewich. Walter was a great guy. He had devoted more than 20 years to public life.

As you'd expect, there were many local leaders and celebrities there. Many of

Gordie Tapp

them had a part on the program and it was my duty to introduce them as they were to speak. I did many of the jokes I do all over the world. But the Hamilton Spectator writer didn't like some of the jokes. He was very complimentary of me and the work I had done over the years as an entertainer. He mentioned I had devoted time to helping good causes and that I had been awarded Canada's highest honour, the Order of Canada. But he thought I was politically incorrect in some of the things I said.

That's what I was talking about earlier . . . being able to laugh at yourself.

As I remember, he started off by saying that I made him uneasy when I started a joke: 'Two Jewish businessmen were in a boat . . . '

He said that he noticed other members of the audience - which was more than 500 that night - feel uneasy when I talked about the winners of a flower show being 'Mr. Rose for a bunch of pansies and two pansies for a bunch of roses.'

I think this is harmless stuff, but obviously the writer didn't. A few days later he wrote a column saying that he had had a lot of responses to his column about me. In all fairness to him, he said that the biggest surprise he received was that the comments 'for' and 'against' me and my choice of material for the retiring mayor's event was split down the middle.

You can please all of the people some of the time and some of the people all of the time. But I don't care who you are, or what you do, I don't know anyone who can please all of the people all of the time.

Anyone who knows me knows that the stories I tell are meant to have people laugh at themselves. Of course, other people are going to laugh along with them, but there's nothing malicious in things that I say. Or at least they are not meant to be malicious, intrusive, offensive or racist.

As we live in a society that more and more tries to hide behind the 'politically correct' banner, obviously I have to be more aware of what I am saying - and being very careful to know my audiences. It would be a shame that if people like me, who tell stories about people we share this planet with, are made out to be the bad guy and eventually silenced. I sincerely believe that the only way to fight the racism and prejudice that unfortunately abounds in this world today is through humour. We've got to get more people laughing at themselves and laughing with others. Bullets and bombs are not going to bring us the solutions we'd like to see.

This pencil sketch was presented to Gordie by Jim Pirie in 1965.

Gordie Tapp

Gordie was the subject of many great caricaturists, like this one, by Bob Wood in 1983, in his Naggers skit.

Gordie has a face that cartoonists just love!

Library and Archives Canada / Gordie Tapp Collection

Library and Archives Canada / Gordie Tapp Collection

Gordie Tapp

CELEBRITY ROAST

GORDIE ON TAPP

Paul Benedetti

BURLINGTON'S GORDIE Tapp, known across North America as good ol' Cousin Clem of Hee Haw, is returning to his old stomping grounds tonight as special guest in a roast to benefit the Burlington Visitor and Convention Bureau. It is presented by the bureau and The Burlington Spectator.

Mr. Tapp talks about his long and colorful career with Spectator entertainment writer PAUL BENEDETTI.

Courtesy of The Hamilton Spectator

Gordie's home-town newspaper captured him so well for his Celebrity Roast

197

The Hames Sisters in a skit with Clem in a wheelbarrow.

24

The day Stuie showed up
at Gordie's house with a .38

Another of the characters that I remember so well was an entrepreneur by the name of Stu McLellan. Stu handled programs for most big shows and state fairs in North America, from the Canadian National Exhibition, to the Calgary Stampede, to the Western Provincial Fair in Vancouver, all through the United States, including the State Fairs in New York, California, and Pennsylvania. I worked with Stuie through all those shows, and he was a great character.

I really got to enjoy being with him, and we were working – I guess we were doing a Regina Fair, in those days it was called Buffalo Days, I think they have changed it now. We had a two o'clock show in the afternoon, and I went in early to see that all my stuff was there and everything was ok, and Stuie said 'Let's go to lunch.'

Stu was what we called a 'Cokeaholic.' He had a Coke in his hand most of the time. Rather than booze it was a Coke with him. Anyway, we went to lunch, and when we came back we were in the convertible driving into the fairgrounds and making our way to the parking area at the grandstand. There were two guys in front of us, young guys, also in a convertible. They were talking to the girls and wouldn't get out of our way.

The day Stuie showed up with a .38

Stuie honked the horn and a guy turned around and said 'Ok old man, knock it off.' Stuie got out of that car and just flew into a rage. He grabbed that kid by the scruff of the neck and he pulled him up, shook him and slammed him back in his seat. Stuie said 'When I say you get out of the way, you get out of the way.'

And he came back in the car and the kids got out of the way and I said 'Stuie, you're crazy. You're going to have a heart attack some day. You don't need that kind of aggravation.' But that's the way Stuie was. However, we had a great association through the years.

I worked many fairs for him. He's gone now, but he lived out in La Costa, California.

Stuie once booked me into the Canadian National Exhibition in Toronto. He had Johnny Cash on as well as me. At the end of the week he had Tom Jones coming.

We had a fellow – and I won't mention any names – he was kind of a liaison between Stuie and the CNE board. He worked for the exhibition board. He and I flew out to Nashville and I introduced him to Johnny Cash, because Johnny had done *Hee Haw* several times and we worked on the road together. I also introduced him to a couple of female acts, that he was to use later on.

Johnny and I did our show at the CNE on Thursday night and Tom Jones came in and played Friday and Saturday. But there was some kind of a problem - there was a lot of money missing. I talked to Stuie about it, and he said "There's quite a lot going on here. There's around $250,000 missing in the payment account to Tom Jones." He said there are a lot of accusations going around, people being accused, and so on.

I was certainly glad I wasn't involved in that. I don't know how it worked out in the end, even if the missing money every surfaced.

Stuie was funny. We used to have a party once a year, at the farm, around the pool. One year we had steaks on the barbecue and eggs. We used to serve a glass of champagne in a tall glass with a peach in it. And we would pick the peach with a fork. Then we'd fill it with champagne and you had champagne all through the meal.

At the end of the meal you took the peach out and had it as a dessert, and it was really quite intriguing. We enjoyed it.

While I was doing the steaks, Helen came to tell me I was wanted on the telephone. It was Stuie, and he said "What are you doing?" I said "We're having a little party with eight of our friends." He said "Would you mind if I came over?" And I said "No, Stuie. Come on." Helen looked at me and said "You can't invite him." I said "Honey, it's Stuie. We worked together, let him come."

Anyway, he arrived in a limousine. He gets out and he comes in the kitchen. He knew Helen because we'd met before. And we talked and I said "Take off your coat and relax. We're going to go out and have steak and eggs." So he took off his coat, and he had a .38 in a holster strapped under his coat. And I thought Helen was going to have apoplexy; she just staggered. And I said "You'd better give me that Stuie." And I took it off him and hung it over the chair and put his coat over. Out he goes to the party.

Helen said, "We can't have him here, why would...?" And I said "Helen, it's Stuie, just let it lie." So he stayed, I would say, until 2:30, and the limo came and picked him up.

As he's getting in the car, I said, "What was wrong, Stuie?" And he said "I don't know, I thought I was being followed, and I thought I would be safe out here." I don't know what he was involved in, but he seemed a great guy, and he was always good to me. I made a lot of money with Stuie booking shows.

Sworn-in as a policeman

Gordie, wearing his Sheriff's badge with pride.

25

Sworn-in as a policeman

One day, when *Hee Haw* was doing well, I got a call from the Sheriff's office. They said, "Gordie, we know that you're a Canadian, do you have any interest in American politics?" I said, "I know you've got Republicans and Democrats. That's about all I know."

They said, "Well, we're having a big do at the fair grounds on Saturday night and the Sheriff would like you to act as Master of Ceremonies. Roy Clark's going to be there, along with some other show business dignitaries." I said, I'd love to do that. So they phoned me back and said, "You're staying at the Ramada Inn." I said, "Yes I am." He said, "There'll be a squad car at the Ramada Inn at six o'clock." I said, "To pick me up?" "No, we're leaving the squad car, the keys will be at the reception, bring it out to the fairgrounds, you'll be told where to park."

So I went in on Friday, walked into my dressing room, and there is a Sheriff's outfit hanging up. So I said to my wardrobe mistress, "Am I wearing this on the show?" "No, that's yours, it was brought here by the Sheriff's department, it's yours. You wear it Saturday night." So I went out, and I'm in the studio, waiting around to do my bit, and the producer came over and said, "Gordie, there are two men to see you." I turned around and it was two Sheriffs.

I said, "What's the problem fellas?" They said, "We've got a warrant for you

Sworn-in as a policeman

The strong arm of the law captured Gordie on a Canadian Forces tour on the Sinai Peninsula and charged him with impersonating an entertainer!

Mr. Tapp, you'll have to come down to headquarters." I said to Sam Lovullo, our producer, "Is it alright?" He said, "I can't do anything about it. If you're under arrest, you're under arrest."

They took me back downtown, fingerprinted me, photographed me, and then they took me down the row of cells to put me in a cell. As we were walking down, all the guys in the prison were laughing and yelling, "Hey, Tapper!" "Hey, *Hee Haw.*" When we got down to the cell door, I said, "Guys, is this a gag, or is this for real? What's going on?" They, said, "Nahh, we're just kidding with you, Gordie, you can go back to the studio. We'll have a car drop you off. We just wanted you to get acquainted with the Sheriff and know that Saturday night we're looking forward to . . . blah! blah! blah!"

Anyway, Saturday came, and I put on the uniform, got in the car, and on the way to the fairgrounds I had the siren going. I had a great time.

Can you imagine this happening in Canada? They made me a Deputy Sheriff, they had my picture, they gave me a warrant, called a capias warrant to arrest the guy we were looking for. The capias warrant allowed me to carry a pistol - a .38 - across the state line. All I had to do was show my badge. I never did, but I could have done it. They're amazing people, they really are. That was Davidson County, Nashville, Tennessee.

I was driving back from my uncle's place in Sebring, Florida, and we always used to come the back way. All of a sudden, we've got the flashing lights. I pull over, the officer comes up and I said, "what's the matter officer?"

"Well, you were speeding."

I said, "How do you know officer?"

He said, "Well, I have you on radar."

"Well." I said, "My radar's sitting right next to me and she never said anything about me speeding."

I said, "Don't stand there."

He said, "What are you talking about?"

I said, "You're standing where there are fire ants. Go around to the other side of the car and I'll come out."

I got out and he said, "God damn, you're right, they're here, aren't they?" He was shaking his feet. Whenever you get off the road in the country you're into fire ants.

We talked and I said, "Furthermore, I wouldn't be speeding because I'm an officer of the law." He looked at me and said, "What do you mean?" Well, I took out my badge and showed it to him. He said, "If that's the situation, I won't arrest you, but I'm going to give you a card. I want you to take this to the dealer where you got this vehicle and get them to fill it out." So I did, and guess what, the speedometer was eight miles out.

I'd been going eight miles-an-hour faster than I thought I was. I sent the card back and I never heard another word. I never had a parking ticket in Nashville.

Hometown names street to honour Gordie

Gordie poses under the street sign that bears his name in his hometown of Burlington, Ontario. Many of the interviews and stories related in this book were done sitting in a car on Gordie Tapp Crescent.

Hometown names street
to honour Gordie

I guess it means something to have a street named after you, something to make you proud.

My hometown has honoured me in a very pleasant way. This all happened because I had a farm at Appleby Line and the Queen Elizabeth Way in Burlington. I had a good offer for it, from an Italian man that I knew and I noticed that a very short time later they had a street named for him. I was kind of amazed by that so when I was in the mayor's office as the spokesman for Muscular Dystrophy, I said to the mayor, "I see you named a street after the Paletta family."

He said, "Yes, what's wrong with that?"

I said, "Well, I don't understand it. They just bought the land from me."

He said, "You want your name on a street?"

I said, "no, it isn't that, but I think that the Heslops and the neighbours that lived around me for years, should have their names on a street. I think that's important for the history of our area."

Hometown names street to honour Gordie

That was it, I thought, but a couple of weeks later I got a letter from the mayor, it said: "I brought up the naming of the street for you at city council, but they said, 'we can't name a street for him because he's not dead.'"

I said, "Well have you been talking to Jim Snow lately? They named a freeway after him, and he's alive and kicking."

"I'm not interested in that, I really think you should have the neighbours' names in there."

Not very long after that I got a letter that said: "We are willing to name the street after you, we're going to call it Tapp Trail."

I immediately got on the phone, I said, "your Honour, I don't want it called Tapp Trail, because Gordie Tapp hasn't done enough for the community and contributed, let's forget the whole thing."

Nothing was heard about it for several months, then I got an invitation for a big do at the Holiday Inn. They had a lot of my friends from everywhere at the head table, and some speakers.

They handed me a sign that said Gordie Tapp Crescent, and that's the name of the street in Burlington.

It doesn't mean a lot to me, but I think it means a lot to my kids and my neighbours, I guess that's what's important. And, of course, I am pleased.

27

Gordie was asked to run for political office

You know I've never been that much interested in politics. Oh, I take an interest by reading the newspapers and watching and listening to the news, but being involved in politics has never really entered my head.

I think of all the 'jobs' in life, being a politician is one of the most thankless. No matter how hard you try, never was the phrase 'you can't please all the people all the time' more apropos.

With me having the personality that upsets me when people are not friendly towards me, then just about the last vocation for me would be politics.

I was asked to run as a candidate in a federal election in my home riding a few years ago. Flattering though it was, it didn't take me long to say "no thank you."

Oh, I weighed the pros and cons, but that confrontational way of life just would not have suited my soul. Some of my best friends are politicians. I admire them all, no matter what their political stripe. The damned-if-you-do and damned-if-you-don't decisions they face with even the most picayune situations would have caused me a lot of heartache. I don't know how Prime Minister Stephen Harper or U.S. President George Bush can handle their persona as well as they

Gordie was asked to run for political office

do every day when they always have someone or some group taking them to task - and the media right in their face 24/7 doing their job of trying to keep everyone informed. Having the media make fun of you because you shake hands with your children as they go off to school (Mr. Harper) or because you mispronounce some words, like nuclear, incorrectly (Mr. Bush) just doesn't seem right.

I wouldn't last a day in that environment. I just love life and people so much that I couldn't be there arguing my point, defending my position, or arguing with someone else, just for the sake of being political. That's just not me. As I have said I do admire those who take this route to make our community, our country and our world a better place for all.

One of these people is my good friend, Cam Jackson, elected Mayor of Burlington (Ontario) in November 2006 municipal elections. Cam's a career politician. He'd been a member of the Ontario legislature for more than 20 years in my riding of Burlington until he resigned to run for mayor - and for 10 years before that he was on the public school board.

Cam was in the opposition in Ontario when he resigned and had more portfolios in the shadow cabinet of Progressive Conservative leader John Tory than any other member. I believe he had three - Training, Colleges and Universities, Research and Innovation, and Seniors and Long Term Care. I don't know how he does it all.

When he was minister for seniors, when the Conservatives were in power, Cam presented a variety show for seniors every year. For 15 years I've entertained at the show. It's wonderful. Most of the audience are senior people, and of course, as you know, if I entertain it's got to be seniors because the way they live is relative to my way of life.

As a fundraiser every year, Cam has a golf tournament. I play in it and also tell a few jokes during the dinner or the presentation of prizes. It's a great day, I wouldn't miss it.

Cam introduced me to another great guy, Walter Oster, just an amazing man. The three of us get together from time to time - to dine or to fish or just to talk.

Walter is the chairman of the Canadian National Sportsmen's Shows in Toronto, and is one of the officials of the Great Salmon Hunt. We were out on the lake one day and I got a 19-pounder. Of course, a guy in another boat got a 32 1/2 pounder and won a $30,000 boat and motor. That's always the way it was with me; the fish look at my bait and go and grab the other guy's line. Although, catching those big fish in Florida and having that 19-pound salmon on my line, I suppose I can't complain about fisherman's luck.

Just a last word about Walter. John Howard, former owner of Vineland Estates winery, said to me something that I thought was really tremendous. He said "If everybody in the world was like Walter Oster there would never be any problems." That's the kind of guy Walter is; he helps out in everything he can and I've never mentioned a thing to him that he hasn't said "Well, if you want some help with it, I can do it for you." Walter Oster, somebody making a difference in many lives. By the way, I understand PGA golfer, Mike Weir, who grew up in Sarnia, Ontario, is now associated with Vineland.

One last story about my buddy, Cam Jackson, and the sensitivity he has been able to maintain. Cam had a fundraiser in Burlington, and they limoed me to the show and limoed me back to the hotel. Tommy Hunter, was in the audience that night. It had been a while since I had talked to Tommy. At one time we were very close - especially when we were working together every week. But time and circumstances put some distance between us.

I am sure everyone has great buddies at work, but when you move on to another place of work you make new friends. It's not that you don't like them any more, but you get a new circle of friends. That's what happened to me and Tommy. Tommy came over shook hands and talked, asked how everyone was, and sure wanted to know how Helen was doing. (Helen and Tommy's ex-wife were also the best of friends when we were both working at the CBC). I had introduced him to Cam - as if Canada's Country Gentleman needed to be introduced to anyone in Canada. It was good to see Tommy again - and it brought back a head full of memories of those great times we spent together in show business.

So what's Cam got to do with this? Cam, ever walking that fine line between trying to do right for everyone and trying not to upset anyone, knew that Tommy and I had gone our separate ways over the years, and he called me just to make sure that he had not put me in an embarrassing position by inviting Tommy to the event where I was performing.

I assured him he hadn't. I don't know whether Cam called Tommy and asked him the same question. I wouldn't be surprised if he did, that's just the way Cam is - and that's why he has been such a successful politician over the years. Great job, Cam.

Gordie Tapp

Gordie put Puce on the map. It is a little community near Belle River in southwestern Ontario, just outside of Windsor. Gordie was on a bus, returning from a show, when he awoke and asked "Where are we?" Someone said "Puce" and that was it. It sounded funny, everyone was in one of those crazy moods where you laugh at anything and everything, and the name stuck. Gordie's stage partner Alex Reed, known as Barrelhouse Bill, who played a great Honky Tonk piano, named his cat Puce. Then on-stage one night he introduced Gordie as "the ambassador of Puce." This mock newspaper *The Puce Bugle* was made for a show. Gordie started using a newspaper as a prop on the *Ralph Emery Show*. He was looking for something original and decided to read 'the local news' delivering each story with a punch line. This routine has been delighting audiences for decades.

28

The loves of my life . . .

I have some great loves in my life. My wife, Helen and our family, of course are the really special ones. I have been blessed with a beautiful family. When I got married I certainly didn't know the kind of woman I was getting. Young fellas don't even think past the looks, never mind thinking about a future together. That was me.

I have heard guys talk about marrying above their station in life. There's no doubt I did. I married up for sure. But more about that in a few minutes.

You've read about me loving horses. I have had some wonderful horses. I used to raise quarterhorses when we had our first farm in 1962 and 10 years later was lucky enough to have the grand champion quarterhorse at Quarterama in Toronto.

His name was Shoops 'E' Bar and I used him for breeding. His dam and stallion were both Bar horse champions, so when I got Shoops I knew I had something special.

There was a chance I was going to sell him when he won at Quarterama. He was obviously worth big bucks. But someone told me to wait a few months until the Royal Winter Fair at Toronto's Exhibition grounds.

The loves of my life . . .

They thought it would really be worth a lot of money if he did well at the Royal. So I decided to wait. The Quarterama was February and the Royal in November, so it was only eight months. It made sense to hold off selling Shoops.

Well, five-and-a-half months after Quarterama, Shoops died of a twisted bowel, something quite common, apparently, in horses. I was out of town doing a show at the time and I couldn't believe it. It was a sad day for me. Shoops was a beautiful horse. I'd had him two-and-a-half years. Just imagine when you have anything for that long how you become attached to it. It really is like family.

I know I'd been thinking about selling Shoops, but I didn't. I used the excuse to wait for the Royal before selling. But, you know, I don't know whether I would have been able to sell him even if he had won the grand prize at the Royal.

I know it would have been a good business decision. But I just don't think I could get up every morning and go to the barn and not see Shoops there.

It was a shock that he was gone. There is a comradeship . . . or companionship . . . or an esprit de corps . . . that you don't have with a human. It's there. It's real. You feel it. The horse feels it. You talk to them when they're walking and they put one ear back to listen to you, it's a wonderful feeling. I'd shared these feelings with Shoops. Now he was gone.

Another love in my life has been my admiration for the Harley-Davidson motorcycle. I've had five of them through the years and I've ridden them for over 50 years. The first Harley I had was a Toronto Police bike that I had completely rebuilt. It was a shovelhead, silver and black.

Then I got the big model with the fairing and all the accessories. With Harley you can buy a lot of factory accessories as well as others that are developed by Harley lovers.

Another pretty bike I had was the Heritage Softail.

I used to get a kick out of riding my Harley, especially when motorists would drive by in their cars and give me the thumbs-up. I often took this to mean that they wished they could be riding instead of driving.

I don't ride any more, I just don't trust the people on the road today. If I were the only driver on the road I'd probably still be putting on the leathers once in a while and going for a spin. However, I have a lot of motorcycle memories. I

Gordie Tapp

Gordie in the driveway of his home with his pride and joy - a 1958 Dodge Fargo truck. When it comes to enjoying horsepower he is very happy with just a single horse. His favourite was Shoops, who died suddenly after being named the best horse at Quarterama in Toronto. This was the trophy Shoops won.

Gordie Tapp family photo

The loves of my life . . .

Gordie was the voice of the donkey on *Hee Haw* for 25 years.

Hee Haw producer "Sal . . . utes" Gordie

Gordie Tapp . . . a comedian, impersonator, humorist, singer, actor, musician and writer, which makes him a class act.

Gordie came into my life in 1969 when he was called to perform and write on the *Hee Haw* show. We knew of him as an entertainer on a TV show in Canada. He was the right fit for *Hee Haw*.

We can now say he was a huge part of the success story of *Hee Haw*. His creative contributions to the show were immeasurable.

As a writer and stand-up comedian he has had the unique ability to insert a twist to a story and make it funny.

To symbolize his talents – if you want an audience to laugh and clap – call on Tapp!

Never a dull moment with Gordie!

Sam Lovullo
Producer
Hee Haw

The loves of my life . . .

A collection of cowboy boots and Stetson hats - worn over the years both on and off the stage - each have their own memories for Gordie. And in true Gordie Tapp fashion not only is the picture worth 1,000 words, but every subject is worth a joke. So here goes . . .

For the boots story . . . It is Northern Ontario, it is winter, and it is 20-below zero and there's two-feet of snow in the school playground. The teacher spent several minutes getting boots on a little kid. When she was finished, the kid said, "They are not my boots." So the teacher patiently took off the boots and held them up for the entire class to see and said, "Whose boots are these?" And the kid, sitting there in his stockinged feet said. "They're my brother's, but I'm wearing them this year." Isn't that just typical of kids?

And for the hat story . . . I tell about riding into an arena out west on a horse, when my hat blows off in the wind. I would thrill everyone by riding around and picking the hat up with my teeth - and for an encore I would go back and pick up my teeth!

218

miss it, for sure. But you've got to be realistic, I guess.

One story I should tell you about motorcycles . . . When I was 18, I had an old Indian motorcycle. I brought it home and lost control of it and went through the chicken fence and scattered white leghorns throughout the community, then spent until 2 a.m. collecting them all and bringing them back home. My father was disgusted with me because when chickens get riled like that they don't lay eggs that quickly and it was important that we have those eggs.

From two wheels to four - I have had many beautiful automobiles. My favourite was a Mark VIII Lincoln. It was seafoam green. I drove it for four years and when the book value was just over $7,000 I got $13,000 for it. I wish I'd never sold it, but you can't keep everything.

Today I drive a Mercedes, a very nice car that will do almost anything and is equipped with the latest and faddy accessories of the day - GPS, automatic lights, that sort of thing. But it doesn't give me the kind of thrill that the Lincoln did when I stepped into it.

I also have a truck. Now this is my pride and joy. It is a bright red, fire engine red, Ferrari red, beautifully reconditioned 1958 Dodge Fargo. It drives nicely, doesn't use a lot of gas but gets lots of attention from other motorists when I am on the road. They honk their horns and the drivers nod and smile when they pass me - of course, they are doing 65 and I am doing 45. But in that baby it seems like 65.

I don't want to sound as though all my loves have a monetary value. I would be disappointed if you thought that. Boys love toys and I am really no different than the average guy in this respect. I don't think I am extravagant. I am sure Helen would tell me if she thought I was spending money foolishly.

The really important things in life are priceless. You can't put a dollar value on them.

For instance, I love making people laugh - I think that is a great love - and a great ability - of mine. There's nothing more enjoyable than watching people laugh, especially seniors.

There's nothing more rewarding than to walk off the stage to lots of laughter. I always tell the folks when I get a standing ovation that it was exciting and that I appreciate it. Just a short time ago I performed for the International Jockeys Federation in Louisville, Kentucky, and I got a standing ovation, but I didn't know it! I couldn't resist that one!

The loves of my life . . .

My life is busy and exciting. There's hardly any down time. I like it that way. I am blessed that I have the health to live the life that I love.

When you are a busy guy like me you really treasure the quiet moments in life. For me it is away from the camera, off the stage.

I love fishing. At one time, when the kids were young, we had a cottage on Colpoy Bay, in the Georgian Bay area, and I fished every summer.

I've been a boater. I had a boat built by a man named Kalbfleisch on Colpoy Bay which I kept for several years on Georgian Bay. When we bought the farm we sold the cottage and built a big pool on the farm. The kids enjoyed that, the girls were getting to the point where they didn't want to leave and go for four weeks or eight weeks up north and be without their friends. I guess that happens in most families.

All my girls were fishermen. We fished together. When I talk about the quiet of being out on the water in the fresh air and fishing, I am thinking of the tranquil scenes that abound in Ontario. However, when you fish in Florida, in the ocean, when you get a bite it's not that peaceful. You're not dealing with a two or three pound trout, you're fighting a fish that can be 150 pounds - that's as big as a man. The adrenaline kicks in and the battle between man and fish is on. It can take an hour or two to get some of those ocean fish in the boat.

In Florida I had a 38-foot Tournament Fishing Boat. It was diesel-powered, but talk about a fuel-guzzler. However, it was marvellous for what we needed.

I caught a few good-sized fish. My biggest was 148 1/2-pound blue marlin. Another time I brought in a 100-pound tarpon.

The ugliest fish I ever landed was a 50-pound grouper. I brought it back and started to clean it but I realized it was old and the meat was as tough as leather, so I towed it out about 10 miles into the ocean and cut it loose. It wasn't very long before other fish were eating it, just tearing at it.

Now I have a 23-foot centre console fishing boat down there, with a 150 hp Yamaha on it. It gets the job done - gets us where the fish are.

Now to my family. Great kids, great grandkids and now great, great grandkids - what more could a man ask for in life?

Helen is a magnificent woman. She's strong, very strong. Oh, there has been a few times when she got very upset about people I associated with at work.

Gordie and Helen's four children - Barbara and Jeffrey, Joan and Kathleen

Gordie Tapp family photo

The loves of my life . . .

Gordie and Helen have been married for more than 62 years. They both live and act like people decades younger than their 84 years. They love life and particularly love their ever-growing family.

Gordie Tapp family photo

Gordie Tapp

For example, once in a while I'll call Gunilla Hutton, who played Nurse Goodbody on *Hee Haw*. I always close by saying, "I love ya." Helen said, "Do you have to say that?" I said, "Yes, we all loved each other, that's what made us the unit. That made us work together. It isn't love like love, it's just . . . well, love. I can understand people not realizing it, but, you know, show people are the worst for hugging and kissing each other. Men, too.

When I was doing commercials for Ultramatic and I'd be in bed with other women, my wife would say, "You look at her like a cow looks at a haystack." I'd tell her that's what people expect when you're in bed with a woman.

We've been married for 63 years. We both must be doing something right. We both still enjoy each other's company. Helen still laughs at my jokes after all these years. One time she reminded me of the time we went in to see Uncle Herb (Herb Bedford) in the hospital. We knew he wasn't doing very well.

Here was a guy who had been wounded in the arm in World War I. He had a big hole in the arm that he used to fill with water and then float a needle in it. When he was well he always amused me. I didn't know what we were going to find now he was ill.

On the last time we saw him, we walked into his hospital ward and as soon as he saw me he crooked his finger for me to get down near his mouth. He said, "Did you hear the one about . . ?" He died a little while later. He was 92.

My wife says that's how I'll go - telling jokes right to the end.

Well, what a way to go. That would be perfect.

Years ago, back in the full-time working days, I'd be away months and months at a time playing the circuit out west, the fairs in the United States, overseas for the Canadian Forces, and Helen stayed at the farm with our four children. She made it work. In fact, obviously, we both made it work. Mind you, we had some good parties when I got home. We were talking about it the other day, she said, "I used to like the diamond rings you'd bring from Beirut."

That reminded me of some funny experiences coming back and forth through Customs into Canada.

We travelled so much, we had been in Pisa, Italy. I had bought a pair of picture frames. They were beautiful. In fact, we still have them at home on paintings my father-in-law did. He was a fine artist.

These frames were wrapped with burlap. I put them over my shoulder and carried them. The Customs guys all knew me, because I was going through

223

The loves of my life . . .

Customs and Immigration all the time with our trips. They said, "what do you have now Tapp? I said, "you'll love this. I've got His and Hers toilet seats." They said, "get through here and forget it, what kind of nonsense is that?"

I came through one day with a box as long as that car and half as wide. "What's this?"

"It's an airplane."

"What?!"

"It's an airplane Six-foot wingspan."

"Oh, let him through, he's nuts."

Imagine doing that today. Oh, how things have changed . . . for the better or for the worse, that depends on the situation. So many things are so much better, but there are some things - such as airport security, crime and safety in our communities, that have taken away that freedom that we once enjoyed.

I'm not going to go down that road. But you get the picture . . .

In my career I have worked with some of the finest musicians - Peter Appleyard of Benny Goodman fame, Chet Atkins, a country music legend, Phil Nimmons of Nimmons and Nine.

In the country music field Carl Keys, Mel Aucoin. Bobby Lucier, Johnny Bourque, Al Briscoe come to mind.

Making friends seems to be easy, but keeping them is more difficult. Many thanks to all the friends I've kept . . . and I look forward to making new friends as the years go by.

Some friends have said "I hear you're writing your life story, Gordie."

I have to tell them that it's not over yet. This is only my life story to date.

After all, I'm only 84.

Gordie Tapp

As a special thank you for reading his book, Gordie has made this DVD with the assistance and permission of the Canadian Snowbird Association and Christopher Bradbury, Vice-President of Medipac. Because you purchased this book you are entitled to send for this DVD. Gordie wants you just to cover postage and handling. Please clip out this page and mail it to the address at left..

Send $12.95 to:
Tapper Productions
PO Box 627
RR 1
Rockwood, Ontario
Canada
N0B 2K0

Name ....
Address ....
City...
Province/State ....
Postal Code ....
Quantity ☐   Total $ ☐
Please send cheque or money order. Credit Cards not accepted.

Gordie Tapp

ISBN 1425106560-0